Betsy and Hubbard Cobb

CITY PEOPLE'S GUIDE TO COUNTRY LIVING

COLLIER BOOKS, NEW YORK, NEW YORK

The Macmillan Company
866 Third Avenue, New York, N.Y. 10022
Collier-Macmillan Canada Ltd., Toronto, Ontario
City People's Guide to Country Living is also published
in a hardcover edition by The Macmillan Company.

Library of Congress Catalog Card Number: 72-85757

FIRST COLLIER BOOKS EDITION 1973

Printed in the United States of America

CITY PEOPLE'S GUIDE TO COUNTRY LIVING

Your Basic Survival Kit for Happy Country Living

If you'd like to move out of the city or the suburbs but have never lived in the country, you're apt to be filled with doubts, insecurities, misconceptions, and anxieties. This book will dispel many of your fears, tell you how to handle the move, and perhaps give you courage to make the break.

Down-to-earth and packed with information, *City People's Guide to Country Living* will help you plan for your move while you're still tied to the city. Want to know if you'll like rural life? What should you do before you pull up stakes? Will you be able to make a living in the country? Betsy and Hubbard Cobb cover these points in detail, as well as:

- Choosing a house
- Building or renovating a house
- Living off the land
- Making friends
- Getting to know the territory
- Raising children
- Your first garden
- Becoming part of the community
- The woman without a partner
- Wildlife—friend or foe?
- Buying food at harvest time
- Tools and equipment
- Auctions and flea markets
- Lumberyards, hardware, and other supply stores
- Dealing with emergencies

City People's Guide to Country Living is Mrs. Cobb's first writing venture. Her husband, the author of *How to Paint Anything* and co-author of *The Complete Homeowner*, was building editor and editor-in-chief of *American Home* magazine for seventeen years. They live in East Haddam, Connecticut.

CONTENTS

chapter 1
SHOULD YOU MOVE
TO THE COUNTRY?

Country living isn't for everyone, and before you make the break from the city, you ought to be reasonably sure that it is for you. If you feel a little hesitant, you're absolutely right, because there are indeed risks—both economic and psychological—in leaving the familiar and moving into a strange and new environment. Especially if the move means giving up a good job, with possible pension plans and other fringe benefits. Along with the job, there are also psychological fringe benefits you will be leaving: good friends, favorite places to eat, drink, and shop, all kinds of cultural advantages—and that part of your ego which may be far more dependent on your status and job title than you realize.

Some people shouldn't even think of moving to the country—it just wouldn't work. For instance, if you think of all country people as bumpkins, country ways as dumb or tacky, and country quiet as a frightening silence, you're probably among those who should stay in the city. If you don't care for gardening, can't drive a car and are not fairly handy with your hands, you're going to feel lost in the country. If you cherish the anonymity of the city and think you're being neighborly if you nod to the people in the next apartment, you won't like the feeling that everybody knows who you are—even if you don't know them—and that neighbors keep an eye on each other's comings and goings.

You won't like the country if you are easily bored—there are long stretches when not much happens. Or if you are a "night" person—country people go to bed early and get up early. If the city is really in your blood, and you feel it is the only place where the action is, you probably won't change your mind. But if the negatives in the city have begun to outweigh the positives, maybe you ought to give the country a chance.

The best way to test your tolerance to country life is the second home, vacation house, or future retirement home —if you can afford it—living in the city during the week; spending weekends and vacations in your country place. In a sense, this is the best of all possible worlds. You can leave some roots in the city while putting down new ones in the country. This eases the transplanting pangs considerably, *if* and *when* you want to leave the city entirely. Doing it slow and easy also gives you time to really get to know an area, make friends, and look into job or business possibilities. Not everyone is affluent enough, or hardy enough, to be able to hedge the bets like this. Sometimes you just have to take the plunge.

We tried this somewhat schizoid way of living for a while, and in some ways, it was very pleasant. Maintaining two places turned out to be surprisingly expensive, though, and eventually, driving back and forth every weekend became too much of a strain—especially on Bruckner Boulevard. Then there was the laundry problem. Shall we take it back to the city and have it done? Or shall we buy a washing machine? We bought the washing machine. What's in the refrigerator? Two pounds of butter at one place sometimes; none at all at the other. Shall we go out to the house this weekend? We really don't feel like it, but if we don't go, we'll feel guilty or worry—especially in cold weather when there's always a chance the furnace will conk out, the pipes freeze, and all the rest of it.

After a couple of years, we decided for various reasons —one of them being that the rent on our apartment had just been raised *again*—that we could not afford the luxury of living in two places. Especially since we were no longer living a salaried existence. What to do? Give up our place in the country? Unthinkable. Give up the apartment and try free-lancing in the country? Let's try it! So we tugged that final root out of the city cement, and holding our breath, we made the transplant. And we're very glad we did.

It helps, of course, if you have lived in the country before. We both had the experience as children, and from time to time during our adult lives, so we had some idea of what to expect. And we did, by that time, have the house in reasonable living condition. Even if your country experiences have been limited, if you are fairly self-reliant, have one handyman (or handywoman) as a member of the family, like the outdoors and the idea of making things grow, don't mind working hard, and don't have a pressing need for constant outside stimulation—you can make country life rewarding and certainly healthier.

Almost everybody in the country works hard. If they're not working at one job, they're moonlighting on another. If they're not moonlighting, they're fixing the roof or painting the barn or chopping wood. And once in a while they take a day off and go fishing. Farmers—and writers —work the hardest of all. It makes no difference if it's back country, small-town country, or outskirts-of-a-small-city country, most people have to scratch to make a living—whether it's farming, working in a factory, selling real estate and insurance, driving a truck, teaching school, or minding the store. In some parts there are more blue collars than white, and a sprained back is more serious, and more common, than a nervous breakdown. Pick-up trucks are more prevalent than station wagons and so are women driving them. And there are a lot more 4-H Clubs than country clubs—or Twenty One Clubs.

You have to get used to doing things for yourself in the country. Many of the conveniences and services you are used to in the city or the suburbs just aren't available. If you want some clothes dry-cleaned, you take them to the cleaner's—not the other way around. The corner druggist won't send up your prescription if you're in bed with the flu, because there probably won't be a corner drugstore within five miles—and even if there were, they wouldn't deliver. Your friendly liquor store will not make house calls, and there's no Chinese restaurant to send up a hot meal at a lift of the phone—although there just might be a Colonel Sanders or a pizza parlor a few miles away. But you still have to go out to get it. The local grocery store doesn't make a habit of delivering, either, but in a pinch—if you're not too far away—they might do you a favor once in a while. Especially if somebody happens to pass your house on the way home, and you don't ask too often.

On the other hand, shopping for basic household needs can often be a lot easier, simply because there aren't as many people around competing for the salesclerk's attention. Of course, you don't have the selection you do in the city, but it's surprising how little difference this makes, except in certain instances, such as highly styled clothing or some luxury items. And you certainly won't need much of that sort of thing. There are plenty of work clothes around, which is what you'll wear most of the time, anyway. Then there's always mail order, which is a big thing in the country. If you can get your hands on a Sears Roebuck catalog—and they're not that easy to get—you're all set.

A car is absolutely vital. And if it's a station wagon or a mini-bus, so much the better, because you'll need the space for hauling all sorts of things. If you can afford two cars, a pick-up truck is a handy second, but whatever style car you have, keep away from one with temperamental insides, unless you're a car nut and can fix it yourself. The service station may be a good piece away; there probably won't be any buses, and if there is a taxi service around, it'll cost you an arm and a leg. (Just like in the city, except there aren't as many of them and distances are greater.)

You're going to have to depend on yourself for a lot of things, including fixing things around the house if something goes wrong. There's no "super" downstairs to come when you call, and the General Handyman, like the General Practitioner, seems to have gone out of style. The local plumber will come and so will the local electrician, but usually in their own time. What seems a real emergency to you may seem fairly minor to them, and since there are not all that many specialists around, you don't have much choice but to leave the setting of priorities up to them. So bring your own library of fix-it-yourself and how-to books plus—hopefully—a little basic knowledge of what makes a house tick. And if you don't know what a plumber's friend is, maybe you better find out before you need one.

You'll also have the pleasure and responsibility of disposing of your own garbage (there's no Sanitation Department making daily rounds) and the "dump" which may serve your village may also serve four or five others in the area and might be fifteen or more miles from where you are. There are usually waste disposal services around somewhere, or perhaps a local farmer who moonlights in the garbage business, but you'll have to pay for the convenience.

Entertainment, also, must often be self-generated by you and your family. This may or may not be a good thing, depending on how imaginative you are. Even so, it is nice to be able to go to a movie once in a while, and if you have one in your town, consider yourselves lucky. Where we live, the nearest movie house—eight miles away—burned down last summer, and the next nearest one was sold to a supermarket. The one where we do go occasionally is fifteen miles up the line, but they do have pretty good movies from time to time. Things are apt to be somewhat more lively come June, if there are summer theatres in the area, but in winter, unless you start your own Little Theatre Group, you either read or turn on the TV. And if you think the programs are terrible in the city, wait until you sample country fare, where the only two channels you'll often be able to get offer movies so crummy or so old that even a ten-year-old can't be bothered. If you don't have CATV, how many times can you look at "The Golden Horde"? Of course, if you live near a college or university center, there's a lot more going on in winter—lectures by visiting pundits, plays, concerts, art exhibits, and maybe even a few encounter groups. (If they'll let you in, and you choose to participate.) Otherwise, winters can be somewhat barren, especially if you're a new settler and haven't yet—or don't want to—become involved in local politics, church activities, fraternal and civic organizations, and so on. If you have children in the local schools, you probably won't have this problem, because you'll no doubt be involved in the PTA and other school activities.

In winter, if you live in snow country, much that you do outside the home will depend on the condition of the roads, and sometimes you don't have much choice but to stick close to the hearth. But it's surprising how intrepid you become after awhile if you really want to go somewhere, even if you're a fairly timid driver. In many areas the roads are well sanded, because people simply have to get to their jobs. And pretty early in the morning, too, because the work day starts at 8:00 A.M. or earlier.

Things have changed considerably since the advent of the snowmobile, too. With this form of recreation, a lot of nonskiers have found something to do in winter, and the voice of the "Thing," which has been likened to a cross between a buzz saw and a six-foot mosquito, is heard, in ever-increasing numbers, throughout the land. The increasing popularity of snowmobiling has created a good deal of dissension and ill feeling between the Pros and the Cons. The Cons include many conservationists who consider the practice nothing less than ecological rape. You might keep this in mind if you're heading for the hills or the prairies. You'll probably have to choose up sides.

The weather will become very important in summer,

too. Not only as it affects your garden or crops, but as it affects your water supply. Your well—and you'll undoubtedly have one unless you're close-in and there's a town water system—can, and sometimes does go dry during a long period of no rain. In that event, you'll have to haul water—which is no fun. You'll also have to haul water if the power goes off after a bad storm, or if there's a power shortage. We don't want to worry you unduly, but sometimes a power shortage or knock-out can last for several days. If this happens in hot weather, you start to worry about your food spoiling—and a freezer full of food gone bad can hurt. If it happens in cold weather, you don't worry about the frozen food—you worry about the frozen people—because as the power goes, so goes the heat. Candlelight and kerosene lamps may have been adequate in Mr. Lincoln's day, but if you're used to electricity, it's not quite the same.

Neighbors are very important in the country. And it's to everybody's advantage to get along with one another. You don't have to be chummy, but you certainly want to be civil, and once you get to know each other, you might even be friends. Your country neighbor can very likely teach you a lot—more than you can teach him—and the one thing you don't want to do is to make the mistake of treating him like a hick. Country people have plenty of self-respect and are not too impressed by money or the fact that you may possibly have a superior education. Maybe you do and maybe you don't, but you're in their territory now, and it helps if they're on your side.

The decision as to *whether* you should move to the country is one only you and your family can make. *When* you make the move depends on your financial situation, your work prospects, and how strongly motivated you are. If you can do it while you're young, all the better. You do have more energy, pick up new skills more quickly, and if you have to scrimp and save and rough it a bit in the beginning, it's not as much of a hardship as when you're older. Also, if you're young enough, and you find that country living isn't for you after all, you still have time to put down roots elsewhere. Youth, however, is not a basic requirement. Some people are old at twenty, others are as vital and aware and full of wonder at seventy as when they saw their first butterfly. And there are precious few butterflies in the city.

The people we know who have made the most successful transition to country living are those who had positive reasons for moving, other than just escaping whatever phase of city life had become most abhorrent to them. They wanted to do things that they could only do there, whether it was goat farming, organic gardening, breeding dogs, nature photography, running a country newspaper, having more time to spend with their children, or just "being" in the country. All of them have in common a love of the outdoors. They like the simplicity of country living, the fact that they don't have to spend a lot of money on clothes and that entertaining is simple and informal. Most of them have vegetable and flower gardens and raise a good deal of their own food. Some of them fish, hunt, swim, go crabbing, ski, golf, play tennis, go camping, take trips. The richer ones take longer trips—and more often—than the poorer ones. Most have to make a living, and often the work-to-pleasure ratio is a little heavy on the work side; doing first the "bread labor," as author Scott Nearing calls it: the work you do just to keep the actual roof over your head—yard work, the garden, maintenance work on the house and outbuildings, tending any animals you may have, the running of the household. Then there's the "professional work"—Nearing's term for what you do to earn the money to keep the whole thing going. It all adds up to keeping pretty busy. But if the country is for you, just the fact that you are there will be enough. And if you ever feel the slightest bit sorry for yourself, all it takes is a quick trip back to the city to reassure you that you did the right thing.

chapter 2
HOW WILL
I MAKE A LIVING?

Probably not by farming—as we discuss in a later chapter. But there are ways to earn a living in the country, either from your home, by using your land in ways other than farming, by taking a job, or by opening your own business —whether as a professional, a merchant, or by offering a service.

It goes without saying that there are fewer job opportunities in the country than in the city. And in certain rural areas, they can be few and far between. Nonetheless, in many, many small towns, and in or near small cities, your talents, experience, and services may very well be needed. Sometimes, even urgently so. The trick is to find something you can do and like to do in the place you want to live. There must also be a reasonable demand for what you have to offer. It wouldn't make much sense, for instance, for a man or woman trained in criminal law to hang out a shingle in a country village where the crime rate is less than two percent a year. On the other hand, a lawyer who specializes in real estate transactions and handling estates could very well make a comfortable living in the same area.

If you are a lawyer, doctor, dentist, accountant, nurse, or other professional, the search is somewhat simplified because you can check with the various professional organizations to which you may belong for information on out-of-town opportunities. You can also contact state and county professional associations to find out whether there is enough demand for your services in your chosen area to warrant making a move. Professional publications, too, carry advertisements for personnel, as does the Sunday edition of *The New York Times*. There are also employment agencies in the larger cities that cater only to professional people.

Teachers, counselors, librarians, and others in education and the social sciences, also have access to information from professional sources and publications. There are, of course, no guarantees that any of these sources will produce what you want, exactly where you want it. You may, along with most nonprofessionals, have to rely on other sources and data—along with a good bit of leg-work.

Moving to the country is a good time to change careers if you have been dissatisfied with what you have been doing. Or, you may not even want a "career"—just some way to bring in enough money to get by on—leaving you with plenty of time and energy to enjoy the pleasures of living in the country without the strain of pushing for promotions, status, raises, and all the rest of competitive city-style living. Even so, it helps if you have some idea of what you'd like to do and can utilize at least some of your past experience.

Ideally, you already know quite a lot about the area to which you plan to move. You may have summered there, gone to school nearby, lived in the vicinity as a child, or have family or friends whom you visit. On the other hand, you may not know a darn thing about the place, having just fallen in love with it and decided that *this* is the place for you. Whichever is the case, if you have to earn a living, the best time to start learning every possible thing about your future home and the available work opportunities is *before* you make the move.

If there is a medium-sized city not too far away, subscribe to the Sunday edition of that paper—you'll glean a lot of valuable information about what's happening in the whole area. All of this may also spark your imagination about what is *not* happening, and what you could perhaps *make* happen.

By reading the news stories in both the local and the city papers, you'll find out what's going on politically, environmentally, sociologically, and in the business sector. In a few weeks you can get a pretty fair picture of where a particular community is heading. Are commercial enterprises and industry coming into the area or are they leaving? If they're coming in, which ones? There may be good business opportunities for you. If they're leaving the area, you'll want to find out why. Is the area relatively prosperous or is unemployment on the increase? Is the area becoming active as a recreation center or are vacation home communities being developed? If so, there will be a demand for service and other businesses—restaurants, hairdressers, laundromats, gift shops, book and record shops, crafts, clothing, antiques shops and so on.

Read the ads, too. The big ones will clue you in on stores, supermarkets, cultural activities, and movies. But most especially, read the classified ads—there's a lot of meat on those little lamb chops. The Help Wanted section will give you a good idea of salary scales in the area, types of jobs available, and employment agencies, if any. (The Yellow Pages of the local phone book will give you the latter, too.)

Check the business opportunities—see what's for sale and where—there may be a country grocery or hardware store in your future, or a partner wanting to team up with someone like you. Read the real estate ads, of course. Aside from the fact that there may be some property of interest to you, you can learn a good deal about the community from these ads. Are a lot of houses or property being offered for sale in a particular area? If the prices seem low, you might want to find out why. Do these people know something that you don't? Maybe a new highway is going to bypass the community, or the largest employer is moving to another state. Check around and find out. On the other hand, a lot of ads in the Wanted To Buy column means that people have money to spend and that new families are probably moving into the area. (This can be good or bad—depending on whether you want work or just peace and quiet.) Read the For Rent and Wanted To Rent columns. You might have a possible rental unit on your own property that, fixed up, could help pay off the mortgage.

In addition to thoroughly saturating yourself with this newspaper information, you will find a book called *County Business Patterns*, published by the Bureau of the Census under the U.S. Department of Commerce, extremely informative and helpful. The book will give you up-to-date statistical information on all kinds of wholesale and retail businesses, trades, manufacturing companies, business services and so on, in each county of the state in which you are interested. If you want to open a book store, for example, you can find out how many similar operations there are in the county, how many people are employed, and how many taxable payrolls there were in the first quarter of the previous year. The statistics will not only help you analyze the market potential of a given area but also give you a good picture of the industrial structure of a particular region. Just reading the various industry categories alone will probably stimulate your imagination as to what kind of work you might want to get involved in or what kind of business you might open.

Most large city libraries have these books, which are published annually. Along with the latest edition, take a look at those for the past few years. By comparing the figures, you will get an excellent idea of the economic vitality of the county—or the lack of it. If you can't get this book at your library, it will pay you to get it from the Superintendent of Documents, Washington, D.C. 20402.

The cost is only one dollar, and there is an edition for each state.

While it is important to get as much factual and statistical information as you can, you will certainly want to back this up with an actual on-the-spot investigation. You can learn a lot just by looking around, and there are local people you should talk to about job and income opportunities. Briefed by your newspaper-acquired familiarity with the local scene, you can ask perceptive questions and have a pretty good idea as to whether you're getting straight answers.

If you are thinking of opening a business, try to have a talk with the editor of the local newspaper to get his reaction to your plans. He or she probably knows just about everything that is happening or about to happen in the area and can give you a realistic appraisal of your chances of success. Introduce yourself to the local banker, too. Like the newspaper editor, the banker keeps a close eye on the economic health of the area and can be very realistic—sometimes brutally so—about your prospects. While the bank may want you as a potential depositor or borrower, if the banker thinks you'll starve to death or go broke in six months, you'll be told.

The local Chamber of Commerce is another stop to make. The picture painted may be somewhat rosier than the actual one, but you can get considerable basic information from them. Talk to the real estate brokers, too. They know a lot about what's going on—who's moving in, who's moving out, what businesses are looking around for space and so forth. This picture may also be a bit rosier than the facts bear out, but if you ask enough pointed questions, you should get direct answers. After all this preliminary investigation, you ought to have a fairly well-rounded picture of the community and know whether you want to settle there. If you plan to open a shop or start a business, you should also have a good idea of where your clientele is coming from and whether there are enough people to sustain the business year-round or just season-ally. If it's just a seasonal situation—no matter how busy you are during the season and no matter how much profit you make—you still may need some kind of auxiliary income the rest of the year. One woman we know runs an antiques business from her home for about six months of the year, but the other six months are pretty lean. She happens to be an exceptionally attractive woman and, not much to our surprise, we happened to run into her at a local restaurant a few weeks ago where she is established as a combination bartender-hostess for the winter months. This sort of thing is pretty much taken for granted in the country, and nobody thinks anything of it. Come June, she'll be back in the antiques business. And because she has lived in the area for several years, she probably won't have any trouble getting another job next winter should the restaurant not need her services.

As a newcomer to a community, you will not have the advantage of friends in the area, so if you are job hunting, it's a good idea to have a resume of your background, experience and credentials, just as you do in the city. If you're a young person without much experience, bring your resume with you when you talk to prospective em-ployers. If you're somewhat older and are looking for an executive spot, it's a better idea to either send your resume in before the personal interview, or afterwards, along with a covering letter thanking the individual for the opportu-nity to talk with him. This gives him a chance to study the resume at length and perhaps to check some of your refer-ences.

The prospective employer may not be as impressed with your salary and the titles you have acquired along the way, as with what you have done and your general manner in presenting yourself. Don't make the mistake of trying to impress him, or her, with your Big City know-how. He may already be a little leary of you as a city slicker. If you can tactfully emphasize your experience without hitting him over the head with it, you may make a friend, and you may gain an employer.

Sometimes city ways of doing things are readily accepted in the country, and sometimes an idea that seems pretty fabulous to you doesn't get to first base. You may, for instance, have all sorts of good ideas as to how a company could expand its business, but you have to be sure that this is what the company wants to do. An acquaintance from Chicago, a former sales manager for a large company there, had vacationed in our area for some years and had fixed his eye on a small, family-owned company a few miles away, ever since he had learned that they made a certain nationally distributed toilet article. The company had been in business for about seventy years, and the product was a good one, made exclusively by them. Our sales manager, eager to make a business connection in an area where he had decided he would like to live, decided that the company hadn't nearly begun to tap its potential in the toiletries field. He made a thorough study of the whole operation, got together a lot of marketing information, then had a visit with the company's president, outlining his plan whereby the company could double its sales in a year. The president listened politely, then announced that they weren't interested in more sales or more money. They liked things just the way they were—everyone was making enough without having to work too hard, and he couldn't see what they would do with more business except worry about it. Our aghast sales manager went away feeling that the company was downright un-American.

None of which means that the idea was necessarily a bad one. What it does illustrate is that perhaps the sales manager should have done a bit more local research into the attitudes of the company before he spent so much time and effort on the project. It is also true that some established communities not only don't want anything to do with "progress" or change of any sort, but resent anyone else, especially a newcomer, who makes any attempt to change the status quo. On the other hand, if a community has been having rough economic sledding, they may be extremely receptive to new ideas, especially if it means bringing in a new industry or a new business that will employ the local townspeople. And if there are new businesses in the area, there are apt to be more opportunities for you, too. The catch is, that if the place becomes too active and too many companies find the area attractive, you may be forced to look for greener—and quieter— pastures. So while you're doing your research, it may pay you to try to find out what limits, if any, have been placed on expansion.

College and university towns can be pleasant and stimulating places in which to live or be near, and they also offer numerous job opportunities other than teaching. They need administrative and supervisory personnel, admissions officers, secretaries and other office workers, librarians, housekeepers, food workers, custodians, garden and landscaping help, accountants, and public relations people.

They also require service businesses of all kinds in the town itself, including print shops, stationery, book and record stores, photo supply and camera shops, cleaning establishments, clothing stores and, of course, all kinds of restaurants and eating places, plus motels and other places for parents and other visitors to stay. They also need service stations, car repair and service shops, and, seemingly, quite a few secondhand furniture stores, where students can buy and sell their room and apartment furnishings.

Service businesses can be very lucrative, but they require a lot of hard work and often have to be open at least six, if not seven days a week, which doesn't leave you much time for country living. And dealing with the public gets to be a real grind, unless you just happen to be the kind of person who thrives on this sort of thing. Perhaps the hardest business of all, from what we have observed, is the restaurant business, which not only takes considerable know-how, but hours and hours of work, preparatory to the actual cooking and serving of the food.

We once had a delicious dinner in an attractive small restaurant and, as we were finishing our coffee, the host—who was also the owner—sat down to chat with us. He was crisp and cool in his summer sports jacket and had a nice tan. He told us how much better he liked the restaurant business than his former job in an advertising agency. He also mentioned that his wife was responsible for the quality of the food and that, if we could stay a few minutes longer, he'd like to have us meet her. We waited and pretty soon the restaurant was empty except for ourselves and our charming host. Then out of the kitchen came this tired-looking, bedraggled little woman, sweat pouring down her face, her hair tied up in a dishcloth. It seemed that they divided the work—he ran the business end and acted as host, and she did the marketing, prepared the food, cooked it, and washed the dishes. This lady didn't have much time or energy left over for country or any other kind of living. So watch it. You don't want to end up in the same old rat race you left the city to get away from.

chapter 3

BEFORE YOU CUT
THE TIES THAT BIND:
THE PERILS OF BEING
SELF-EMPLOYED

If you are planning on quitting your city job, moving to the country, and striking out on your own, be prepared for some rough sledding for awhile—unless you've got a nice fat independent income. For in spite of the lip service paid to the "good old pioneer spirit" and to the rugged individualist, it's the organization men and women who are the darlings of our economy and the ones who get all the "fringe benefits." The self-employed are looked upon with a certain amount of suspicion.

When you leave a salaried position, you leave a lot more than a desk, a telephone, carefree weekends, and a paid vacation. You also leave:

A Regular Salary: Self-employed people not only have to work hard for every nickel they earn, but they quite often have to wait a long time to get paid. It's quite common with the self-employed to be owed several thousand dollars, by huge corporations, and not have enough money in the family checking account to pay the grocery bill.

Credit: Just as soon as you leave a salaried position, your credit rating takes a nose dive. It's an easy matter in this day and age to borrow far beyond your means if you have a salary, but if you are self-employed, it's a different ball game.

Health and Hospital Insurance: You'll find it more difficult to get the same degree of coverage that you had when you worked for an organization. Also, as an individual or a family, you'll pay much more than when you were part of a group. What's more, you'll have to pay for your insurance in pretty big hunks, instead of having it taken out of your salary in small amounts every pay day or at regular intervals.

Social Security: You'll still have to pay this. However, you'll have to pay more on the same income than you did when you were employed, because you won't have an employer to share the cost with you. And if you make over $7,500 a year, the bite is going to be over $600.

Pension And Retirement: The only pension and retirement plan you'll have is one that you set up, and you will be the sole contributor. When you become self-employed, you should figure on keeping at work until you die or get rich. The former will probably happen before the latter.

Someone To Pass The Buck To: When you are self-employed, you had better be prepared to be able to do everything that needs to be done—right down to licking your own stamps. And if anything goes wrong—if the stamp falls off—you are the only one around to blame.

Being Part Of An Organization: Being self-employed is often lonely. There is no one to shoot the breeze with on the company's time, no nice, long lunch hours with fellow workers, and no expense account. Every hour you waste is coming out of your own hide and your own pocketbook.

Sick Leave: If you are sick when you are self-employed, you don't work, and if you don't work, you don't earn any money. Self-employed people can't afford the luxury of being sick or even having a minor accident that would reduce their efficiency.

Prestige: When people ask you what you do and you tell them that you are self-employed, they're apt to look embarrassed and look away as though you were standing there naked. Until you get really going and start making money or a name for yourself, you just have to have a sense of humor about this sort of thing.

This gives you something of an idea of what it's like out in the cold, cold world of the self-employed.

What does it take to make a success of being on your own? That depends, of course, on what you are doing and how well you do it. It's obvious that if you decide to be a photographer and can't take a decent picture, or a writer who can't write, things are not going to turn out very well. Or, if you decide to start a business that no one needs, or don't have a head for running a business, you are heading for a disaster.

But assuming that you do get involved with something that you can do and for which there is a demand, there are also other factors to consider.

Your Health: You should not try something on your own unless you are in good health and also have the energy that is required to get your project moving and keep it moving.

How Hard Will You Work: Compared to being self-employed, working for a salary is almost like having a paid vacation. Self-employed people think nothing of working ten or twelve hours a day, seven days a week, and they have to be prepared to do everything from keeping their own books, and doing their own filing and correspondence to cleaning up their own office or workshop.

Do You Have Plenty Of Self-Discipline: To make good at being self-employed you have to work hard, and you'll have to supply all the discipline required for this effort. This isn't always easy—and is especially difficult if you are working at home where there are all the usual distractions, plus the temptation on a fine day to go out in the garden or take a walk. Free-lance work is something you have to keep pushing all the time. When you've finished with one job, there's always another staring you in the face. And if there isn't—that's when you'd better start to worry.

There is also the temptation to waste time and energy in the pursuit of the "big deal" that you feel can make you rich. Self-employed people are constantly being tempted by some character who has an invention he'd like to get help with getting off the ground, or a real estate deal or some other will-o'-the-wisp. You can waste a lot of time on these projects, and when you are self-employed, time is just the same as money.

If you should decide to try being self-employed, you should plan your moves *before* you quit your present job.

Use And Get Credit While You Can: As credit is going to be hard to get after you leave your job, use it while you still have it. The time to get a mortgage to buy a house, finance a new car, or make improvements on the house is while you still have a regular salary. This is also the time to establish credit at local stores and other places where you may need it. If you are going to need credit cards— get 'em now. When you have a regular salary, they toss credit cards at you like popcorn, but when you don't have a job, they can be hard to come by. We know one self-employed individual who has written five times for a gasoline credit card and hasn't yet had a reply.

Buy Equipment: If the work you are going to get into involves materials that cost money, lay them in while you have a regular income to pay for them. We know one artist who spent the year before leaving his job with an ad agency buying the supplies he would need for the first year on his own, because he realized that he probably wouldn't be making much money and would be hesitant about buying expensive supplies.

Figure How Much You Have To Earn: Make a list of all your obligations and what it will cost you to live. This should not only include the basics like food, clothing, medical, payments on the mortgage, and insurance but everything—alimony, dog food, and insecticide. When you total these up, you may decide that you can't make enough money on your own to cover these fixed expenses. In this case, you stay put. But if you do decide you can make a go of it, proceed to the next and final step.

Build Up A Cash Reserve: No matter what work you get into, you simply must have enough reserve cash available in the beginning to meet your living costs and fixed expenses. You also need a reserve to tide you over those periods when you're waiting to be paid for work already done, or when there is no money coming in—which does occur. To be happy and self-employed, we'd suggest that you have enough reserve in cash or securities to cover your fixed expenses for at least one year. This is certainly essential in the beginning, especially if you are getting into a new line of work and aren't sure how long it is going to take before you begin to produce a decent income.

chapter 4
MAKING A LIVING FROM YOUR HOME

There are many more ways to do this in the country than in the city. Some involve the use of your home *and* your land but there are many things you can do just from your house, depending on your past experience and where your interests lie. It is our feeling that most city people, until they have lived in the country for a while, should depend to some extent on the skills and talents they bring with them from their former jobs or avocations. Certainly, unless you have considerable capital or income to fall back on, you should not expect to be able to compete with those who make their entire living from the land—whether your eventual goal is truck farming, beekeeping, running a garden center, or other farm or horticultural pursuits. You may be able to do this eventually, but for the first couple of years you're going to have plenty to do just getting your own home garden in prime producing shape so that you can feed yourself and your family and have some saleable surplus, if you're lucky.

There are all kinds of service businesses you can run from your home, many of them requiring little, if any, capital investment. And, unless you start out in a big way, you probably won't run into any zoning restrictions, even if you live in a zoned residential area. Most communities allow what are called "cottage industries" in these areas, or what are deemed "customary home occupations." These usually include small professional or commercial offices, home industries (as long as not more than two or three outside people are employed), and service occupations, provided that all such uses are secondary to the use of the premises for dwelling.

You may be allowed to have a sign outside your house, but it will have to conform in size to the limits set by the local zoning board. That usually means quite small. Also, whatever you are doing must not create any objectionable noise, odor, vibration, or smoke—or in any way change the essential residential character of the neighborhood. Restrictions also usually apply to automobile traffic, so if your business is such that a lot of cars are coming in and out of your place all day, you'll probably be requested to move your activities to a commercial zone. Regulations vary from community to community, so unless there is absolutely no question that your activities would disturb no one—if you are a writer or artist, for instance—better check with the local authorities and get a copy of the zoning regulations before you get too involved. Running a nursery school, for example, might or might not be considered in violation of zoning restrictions, depending on the community. On the other hand, if you are a teacher and do tutoring in your home, it is unlikely that anyone will object.

Both of these occupations are good ways to make money at home; although a nursery school would require some investment in supplies and play equipment, and you would need a fairly large house with a sizable play area outside. And you should certainly be fond of children and have some background in working with them.

If you have secretarial skills, you can nearly always get work to do at home, because such services are much in demand—city or country. Medical secretaries, legal secretaries, and experienced manuscript typists, especially if coupled with editorial and copyreading competence, are also in demand, especially in college and university towns.

Accounting and bookkeeping are other services that are in short supply in many areas and are particularly adaptable to the home office.

The best way to get started in these and other home occupations is to run a small ad in the classified section of the local paper—and run it regularly once a week or once every two weeks. You don't need a display ad; they're more expensive and often not read as thoroughly as the classified ads, but do change the wording from time to time. If you don't, people begin, after a while, to take the ad for granted and even develop a blind spot to it—or worse, become annoyed that it's the same old thing, and that you have somehow trapped them into reading it. Another reason to run the ad frequently is that people forget to write down the phone number and—when they need it all of a sudden—can't find the ad.

If you have writing, editorial, publicity, or advertising copy experience there are a good many things you can do from your home on a free-lance basis. If there is a small publishing business or print shop in your town, it would be worthwhile contacting them and letting them know that your services are available. Small retail businesses often need professional assistance with their advertising or advice on how to publicize or promote what they have for sale, and so do small manufacturers and industries. In addition to advertising in the local press, a well-written letter (on good looking, but not elaborate stationery) describing your services can bring good results. And, by all means, write out a press release or factual description of what you are doing and send it to the local paper and to those papers within a radius of thirty or forty miles. If you have a black-and-white glossy photograph of yourself, send that along. You can find out by calling the paper whether they have a reporter in your town, and if they do, you might try talking to that individual. If what you are doing is interesting enough, or you can make it sound like "news," you might get a feature story out of it. If you are a writer, or a writer/photographer, you also might keep in mind that if the paper doesn't have a reporter in your area, they might like to utilize your services on a free-lance or so-called "stringer" basis.

If you have been an editor or proofreader, you could let this fact be known in much the same manner. Such skills are not easy to find outside of cities, and there may be far more demand than you ever thought possible. Writers and editors don't have to rely entirely on local needs, of course. You may have many contacts from your city days and still be able to capitalize on them via the mails or an occasional trip to the city. This is apt to be particularly true if you have worked in a specialized field—medicine, ecology, law, metallurgy, plastics, pharmacology, or another speciality. If there are other writers or authors in the vicinity, it's a good idea to let them know that your services are available, because they, too, sometimes need editing, proofreading, or writing assistance.

Experienced commercial artists, art directors, and photographers can also do very well on a free-lance basis, expecially in communities where new business and industry is moving in and in areas where vacation and second-home communities are in the process of development. Again, a well-written letter describing your background and asking for an appointment to show your portfolio can bring good results, and a small provocative display ad in the local press from time to time may also help. Many small and medium-sized companies often have their own advertising agencies, but the agencies are not always on their toes and lack that certain expertise most often found in larger cities. The agencies and the companies, too, are apt to be quite delighted to find such expertise in their own backyards.

There are many free-lance opportunities for good photographers in product photography. This is also an ideal home business. It is surprising how many companies do not have good black-and-white pictures for publicity and advertising purposes—or even for their own files—and how many are still using the girl-in-the-bikini-nuzzling-up-to-the-product approach, whether the product is a monkey wrench or a two-ton tractor. Another wide-open field for photographers, from our own experience, is the prefabricated or packaged housing industry. In a recent book we did on vacation houses, we were really amazed at how hard it was to get good photographs of the finished houses from the manufacturers or from their advertising agencies for reproduction in the book. This goes for the mobile home industry, too. Photographers can also collaborate with writers, editors, layout people, and artists in producing booklets and pamphlets for various manufacturers. A small office of this sort in the home often works very well indeed.

Tucked away in the back of the minds of many people is the dream of running an antiques shop in the country. Whether you can do this from your home depends very much on where you are and the zoning regulations. If you're a mile or more away from a village center, in a more or less rural area, you shouldn't have any problem. But if you are in a residential section, you might very well have to apply for what is called a "variance" from the zoning board, in order to open this or any other kind of shop in your house. And you might not get the variance, or you might have such a battle on your hands that you'll wish you'd never started the whole thing. On the other hand, you might not have any problem at all. Still, if this is your plan, you'd better make very sure *before* you buy the house that you can have a shop in it, or the barn, or wherever else on the property you had in mind. In some towns, certain zones are considered semiresidential, which means that you can live in a house and have a "professional" office there, but not a commercial enterprise.

People's ideas of what is commercial and what is professional differ. One woman we know who bought a house in such a district was not allowed to open a fine antiques shop there but could have opened a beauty parlor or a barber shop! Of course, there are all kinds of antiques shops, ranging from the ones with the junk strewn over the lawn to those carrying only the finest eighteenth-century furniture. In this instance, a variance was applied for, and the woman given permission to engage in a "decorating and design" business, carrying antiques as a sideline. Decorating and design was considered a profession that would not detract from the quality of the neighborhood. Since, even under the variance, our friend would not have been allowed to advertise her antiques except in conjunction with a decorating business in which she was not engaged and did not wish to be engaged, she decided to sell the house and take her antiques business elsewhere.

Running a shop from your home can have certain drawbacks, one of them being that you can never really relax, secure in the knowledge that you won't be disturbed. Any hour of the day or night seems to be OK when the antiquers are out. Another drawback is that you're afraid to leave the house for any length of time, for fear you'll miss a customer. In other words, if the customers come, they're sometimes a nuisance, and if you miss some, you worry about going broke!

From the number of home antiques shops you see in almost every section of the country, it is apparent that quite a few people don't seem to mind this seven-day-a-week open house. If you do, it's a good idea to keep a large "Closed" sign handy and also to include in your ads and other publicity the hours when you are open and days when you are not. Even so, you'll probably still be inconviently invaded from time to time.

If you like old things and like collecting them, antiques can be a lot of fun. While you will probably never amass riches from dealing with them, there is a lot of pleasure connected with the chase, and you sometimes meet some delightful and very knowledgeable people. It helps if there are two of you involved, however, because one person has to be constantly searching for fresh merchandise, while the other minds the store. It also helps if both partners have strong backs, because there is plenty of lifting and tugging, loading and unloading to do, and it isn't always easy to find someone to help. If one or both of you can refinish furniture, you will not only make more profit on your merchandise but be able to sell at a better price than the dealer who has to pay to have things refinished, or who sells things "in the rough." If the furniture happens to be of the highest quality, and a fine example of the period in which it was made, you'll detract from the value if you refinish it. But since such pieces are few and far between in today's picked-over market, you probably won't have to give this much thought.

Whether you have a shop or not, if you like to refinish and repair furniture, you have a ready-made home business, and in most parts of the country, a ready-and-waiting clientele of both the general public and dealers. Good refinishers are as scarce as hen's teeth and can get an excellent price for their labors. There is a demand for chair seat caning, too, but while this is a fairly therapeutic occupation, it is not as lucrative as restoring and refinishing. One good thing about this kind of work, though, is that you don't have to invest a lot of money in stock, and what you earn doesn't have to go right back into fresh stock—which is the trouble with the antiques business, as well as with many other retail operations. Other businesses that are well suited to home operation are slipcover and drapery making and furniture upholstering. There is a fairly steady demand for this sort of thing, especially in summer and vacation communities, where people want a seasonal fresh look for their houses. This makes a good husband-and-wife endeavor, and if you can also have fabric samples from the various wholesale houses from which your customers can order—plus some attractive lamp bases, shades, and lighting fixtures—you can offer a pretty solid package which will appeal to quite a few buyers.

Before you get too far into this one, though, be sure and check zoning regulations for the area.

There are all sorts of arts and crafts that make ideal home businesses, such as pottery, weaving, candlemaking and so on. However, most of these businesses have been mentioned so often in magazines and newspapers that it seems unnecessary to go into them here.

There is always a market, however, for attractive and unusual Christmas decorations, and in some sections of this country there are "Christmas Shops" that are open year-round and carry nothing but ornaments, decorations, and other whimsies for the holiday season. Most of them do a fantastic tourist business—whether it's July or November—and are a good market if you have a talent for making such objects. If you can find enough suppliers and have the desire and the capital, such businesses are extremely lucrative, but you should be prepared to face an onslaught of customers in the tourist season and know how to handle a large inventory of thousands of small items. Because such operations usually involve a lot of traffic, you would almost certainly have to be outside a residential zone, but if you approach it just from the actual making of the decorations, you could certainly do this from your home. Stenciling of trays, lampbases, furniture, and other objects is another way to make profitable use of a pair of talented hands.

Sturdy and colorful toys and children's furniture also find a ready market in most areas, and if you enjoy woodworking and have the hand and eye for colorful and simple (and nontoxic) painting of these things, or have an imaginative knack for making cuddly dolls and animals, you can sell either through local outlets or even branch out into the mail-order business, once you've settled on a few really good sellers.

This brings us to the subject of the mail-order business, an ideal home operation and highly touted as such for a number of years. It's still a great idea, but you can lose your shirt in it unless you really know what you're about. Mail order has been Big Business for a long time, now, and millions of dollars are spent every year in advertising and direct mail solicitation by the pros. Millions of dollars are made, too, but mostly by the big boys. This is not to say that if you have the right items you couldn't have a piece of that pie. However, your approach should be scientific and cautious and you should read every good book you can find about the mail-order business before you spend your first dollar. Good luck—but don't say we didn't warn you.

A good many salesmen and manufacturer's representatives work from home offices. Some carry two or three "lines," others prefer to concentrate on just one. If you have had a sales background and enjoy this kind of work, you might begin making the proper contacts before you leave the city so that you can stake out your territory in the place you want to live. One man we know has a fairly busy schedule as a regional advertising representative for a New York-based magazine and is also a local dealer for a modular home company in a nearby state. Because he can do much of his work by telephone and through the mails, he doesn't have to be away from home more than a couple of days a week. He not only has time to have a nice garden in the summer but, through his building contacts, is able to pick up an older house from time to time, remodel it, and sell it.

People are always interested in good food, and if you are an artist in the kitchen, there are any number of ways to utilize your talents to make a living from your home. Catering is one of them, and depending on where you live and the needs of the people in the area, you can keep busy in both summer and winter. One woman we know, who lives near the shore, puts up delicious picnic lunches for fishing and boating trips. If a good-sized party is planned, she likes a couple of days' notice, but she also keeps individually packaged assorted sandwiches and other goodies in her freezer that can be picked up on the spur of the moment. She will also put on a Texas-style barbecue or a clam bake in other people's backyards—a nice change for the host and hostess to be able to enjoy their own parties without wearing the chef's bonnet. During the Christmas season she caters buffets and cocktail parties, or will cook and deliver turkeys, hams, or whatever anyone wants.

All anyone who can bake good bread, cookies, and cakes has to do is to let that fact be known and they're sold out. Whether people are on diets or not, there still seems to be an insatiable demand for quality home-baked products. We are reminded of "the Danish lady," as we called her, who had a bake shop on the ground floor front of the large frame house in which she lived in a small town on Long Island. The road she was on was a moderately busy one, and she had only a small sign outside the house saying "Danish Bakery." The bake shop opened at 11:00 A.M. and closed at 3:00 P.M., but during those hours there was always a traffic jam outside the house and a constant flow of customers streaming in and out. If she sold out at 2:00, she closed the shop and that was that. She was only open from mid-June through Labor Day, but such were the delights of her coffee cakes, cookies, bread, and pies, that not only did she have no need to advertise, but people were practically begging to buy whatever she chose to sell. This was, of course, the beauty of the operation. She could call her own shots—work hard for three months or so and then do whatever else she wished the rest of the year. We never checked, but assumed from the character of the other businesses on that road that the zoning, if any, was commercial—a point to keep in mind, if you are thinking of a similar enterprise.

This rundown on businesses you can operate from your home is, of course, by no means complete, but is offered in the hope that your own imagination will be stimulated. We can't leave the subject without mentioning the real estate business, however. It sometimes seems as though every third person you meet in the country is engaged in this occupation—and in the right place, at the right time, with the right property to sell, the right person can make a tidy sum. In order to operate out of your home, all states require that you have a broker's license. Even if you want to operate a branch office for another broker, you will still have to meet this requirement. And if you want a broker's license, or even a salesman's license, you must pass the examinations given by the State Real Estate Commission. Courses in real estate procedures are offered almost everywhere. An excellent and basic book on real estate is *Questions and Answers on Real Estate* by Robert W. Semenow, published by Prentice-Hall, Inc. This is available at most libraries and bookstores.

If you start a business out of your home, be sure to check with your insurance agent, for it may be that the type of business you wish to engage in would jeopardize your protection under the standard homeowner's policy.

chapter 5

LIVING OFF THE LAND—
CAN IT BE DONE?

As we said earlier, probably not entirely by farming. But if
you have good land, some know-how and are willing to
work, you should certainly be able to grow sufficient produce in your garden to supply a large part of your diet.
You may also be able to sell some of your surplus. But
unless you can utilize your land in ways other than farming, or go in for some kind of speciality growing, you
should not expect to be able to live off the land without
some other means of income.

It's sad, but true. The day of the small, independent
truck, corn, grain, or chicken farmer is about over. Even
though food prices are high, the small farmer's return on
his labor has declined over the years as his investment
costs have increased. Because of increasing specialization
and technological advances, he is unable to compete with
Big Business—which is what the giant agricultural operations are today—raising food with the same cool efficiency
and management techniques used in the manufacture of
any commodity, and using sophisticated machinery that
takes the place of hundreds of thousands of human hands.

Even farmers who have worked all their lives on land
that has been in their families for generations, and have
thousands of dollars invested in stock and equipment, are
tossing in the sponge. Some are selling off their land to
developers or city people and retiring to mobile homes in

Florida. (We've heard that St. Petersburg is known as a southern county of Maine!) Others are using their land and their talents in ventures more profitable than farming —for raising nursery stock or for garden centers. You can get more for a pot of geraniums than for several heads of lettuce, and it takes less time and effort to raise. Even the sharecropper, who never expected anything but hard work and a subsistence living from the land, has been pushed off the land by the machine.

There is a strong countermovement back to the land among young people and quite a few not-so-young people, who are buying land and small farms all over the country and working—either as single families or in communes— toward a new life style. Some are making it and some are not. Some inexperienced new landowners have ended up with rocky or swampy property that not even a Burpee could turn into a subsistence garden. Others, with the help of Farm Advisors and Extension Agents, good books on gardening, farming, and animal husbandry—and that amazing compendium of tools, techniques, and tips for living outside of our complex society, *The Last Whole Earth Catalog*—have not only succeeded in feeding themselves from what they grow but are finding much satisfaction in the natural way of living. One problem, however, is a shortage of cash and many have to either do some sort of crafts work which they can sell or barter for necessities they can't grow, or take on outside jobs from time to time.

The needs of these young people are modest indeed, compared to the average Establishment family. While you, too, may be prepared to lead a simple life, you must nevertheless be realistic about your needs. There will still be shoes to be bought, teeth to be fixed, taxes and insurance to be paid, utilities, clothing, car maintenance and many other necessities that simply can't be had for free.

So how else can you use your land to bring in money? One thing you might consider, if you have land with recreation possibilities and room in your house or out-buildings for sleeping quarters, is to take in paying guests at various seasons of the year.

One couple we know, with three children of their own, welcome other people's children in the summertime and also at spring vacation. They also take preschool children throughout the year, if parents have to be away for business or other reasons.

Originally city people—the husband was in advertising, the wife a teacher—they bought a large, old farm-house and considerable acreage in New Hampshire. They keep a goat, a pig or two, a cow, several hundred chickens, and every spring they put in a good-sized garden. Visiting children (their limit is six) have a marvelous time and unforgettable experiences. At the farm every morning there is the exciting hunt for freshly laid eggs; they are also allowed to help in the garden, feed the pigs, and take turns riding the goat. Supervised by the older "host" children, they swim and fish for "sunnies" in a nearby pond. They help in the kitchen, set the table, and stuff them-selves with farm-fresh food—especially the mile-high angel food cake made possible by the abundance of eggs and the kind-hearted hostess.

Sleeping arrangements for the children are dorm-style and very simple. If parents want to visit, they stay at a motel a few miles away—not at the farm—but they, too, are invited to have angel food cake and milk, on the house.

There are also some sugar maples on the property, and at the appropriate time in the spring, those children who are fortunate enough to be visiting are allowed to help with the sugaring—from helping to hang the sap buckets to enjoying the taste of fresh, boiled maple syrup poured into new spring snow and eaten immediately.

Incidentally, the "host" children are big 4-H enthusiasts, especially the thirteen-year-old girl who recently won a blue ribbon for her prize pig—quite an achievement for a young lady who had spent most of her life in a sophisticated Westchester suburb. (We go into 4-H Clubs in more detail in the chapter on raising children in the country.)

You don't, of course, have to concentrate on young guests. But if you do, it helps if you have children of your own or some experience working with children.

Some vacation farms or ranches are set up to accommodate entire families—others are geared to a particular age group, profession, or recreation. Writers and artists, for example, often want a quiet, scenic retreat where they can work undistracted for a few weeks or months. If there are hunting or fishing grounds on your property or in the area, you could concentrate on attracting these enthusiasts. Many people just like to get away from the city and enjoy the countryside in an informal, nonresort-like setting and perhaps do nothing more vigorous than bird-watching or hiking. If you are on a lake or river, canoeing or boating could be an additional attraction.

If you can provide simple, hearty meals using your own homegrown produce—perhaps enhanced with home-baked bread and your own jams and jellies—it shouldn't take long to build up a clientele of regulars. (You can also sell your jams and jellies to guests for take-home gifts.)

Small, classified ads placed in publications read by the type of person you would like to attract can start the ball rolling. From then on, word-of-mouth, backed up by an occasional ad, should keep you as busy as you'd like to be. After all, if the stately homes of England can open their doors to tourists to keep the old manor house going— why shouldn't you take in a few boarders?

If, in spite of our cautionary words about farming, you still want to try making some money from the land, you might investigate herb growing. According to our informants, this can be a fairly profitable business, both from the mail-order angle and other retail and wholesale possibilities. Some herbalists have roadside stands or sell from their homes. One that we know runs a small restaurant in

conjunction with herb farming. This is Capriland's Herb
Farm, Silver Street, Coventry, Connecticut 06238. A delightful and fragrant place to visit, where one may lunch
on all kinds of delicious dishes made with herbs—and start
one's meal with a delicate herbal wine punch. During
lunch, Mrs. Adelma Simmons, who runs the farm, gives a
little talk on herbs—the kind that were used in whatever
dishes you are lunching on that particular day, along with
other herb lore. Before lunch, one takes a guided tour of
the gardens, and afterwards, visits the shops in the front
rooms of the house where dried herbs, sachets, spices, and
other products are for sale, along with a varied selection of
books on herb growing. Capriland's is quite well known in
this part of the country because, in addition to all these
activities, they often take space in the better antiques
shows, flea markets, and bazaars, where the fragrant herb
products always attract a good deal of buyer attention. If
you visit Capriland's, be sure to call first for a reservation
if you want to lunch there—sometimes you have to wait a
couple of weeks to get one! They ship live plants and seeds,
and you can write for their catalog, which will tell you
about everything they grow and sell, including books on
herbs written by Mrs. Simmons.

Another place you might check into if you are in the
New England area is the Meadowbrook Herb Garden,
Wyoming, Rhode Island 02898. If you live within a thirty-
five or forty-mile area of the farm, Meadowbrook will
deliver live plants to you, although they do not ship them.
They sell all kinds of herbal toiletries, herb teas, spices,
and seeds.

A very thorough book, written by N. P. Nichols of the
Nichols Garden Nursery, 1190 North Pacific Highway,
Albany, Oregon 97321, called *Profitable Herb Growing*,
will tell you what you need to know to go into the herb
business. The book sells for $1.00 and includes recipes
for herb bread and other goodies. According to the book,
herb gardeners who want to sell their plants and seeds will

require at least an acre of ground to run a profitable operation. And to quote them, "it (herb gardening) holds unlimited opportunities, because you can retail right off your own place, wholesale your products through stores, or use mail-order selling. Gardening is America's number one hobby and that is why selling to gardeners is such a paying field." Nichol's Nursery keeps several colonies of bees to pollinate their herb plants, and they also sell the honey for a good price. According to them, the herbs give the honey a unique flavor, and they say that beekeepers all over the country are planting herbs in bee pastures for this very reason.

Beekeeping, and selling the honey, is another business you might consider. To learn just about everything there is to know about bees, you could send for the *ABC and XYZ of Bee Culture*, over 700 pages of know-how on the subject. Published by A. I. Root Company, Medina, Ohio 44256. It sells for $5.75. A smaller book from the same publisher, *Starting Right With Bees*, will give you a general idea of bee culture. It sells for $1.00. There is also a free catalog.

Raising rabbits, goats, or sheep can also bring in some money and add meat and milk to your own menu. Your County Agent or Farm Advisor can assist you with advice and helpful bulletins. "Raising Rabbits," Farmer's Bulletin #2131, Division of Publications, Office of Information, Department of Agriculture, Washington, D.C. 20505, can get you started in researching the subject. Rabbits make good eating, and there is a market for their pelts. Their hides can also be tanned for clothing, purses, and so on. But you always run the risk of becoming so fond of the critters that you can't follow through to the bitter, but necessary end.

The *Dairy Goat Journal*, P.O. Box 836, Columbus, Missouri 65201—a monthly publication devoted to these droll and bounteously milk-producing creatures—will bring you up-to-date on all phases of the goat world, including equipment wanted and for sale, goats for sale, how to make yogurt and cheese from goat milk and a lot of other things you should know if you decide on goat husbandry. The Journal is $3.00 a year. Your County Agent or Farm Advisor can also give you a lot of pointers on goat raising.

Incidentally, if you're thinking that along with giving milk, you can get your goats to mow your grass, we are told that you will be in for some disappointment. You should raise sheep, instead. It seems goats much prefer shrubbery—usually something you are particularly fond of and may prize. They also like fruit trees, berry bushes, the bark of young trees—anything they can reach. And their reach is higher than you'd think, for like little circus horses, they can dance a pretty jig on their hind legs.

Dairy farming with cattle is a very expensive proposition, and unless you are prepared to invest a lot of money in stock and the most modern equipment, better leave it to the pros. But if you like horses, have experience with them, and have the capital to invest in two or three animals, you might consider opening a stable. One woman we know has a large riding ring on her farm, where she gives lessons to children and adults and also boards horses belonging to others. She has considerable wooded acreage with trails, where the more experienced can spend the day riding and picnicking alone or can hire a guide to accompany them.

If you are a dog lover, but don't wish to make the investment of time or money necessary to breed them, it is possible (if you are out in the country or your zoning laws permit) to have kennels for boarding purposes only. One man of our acquaintance, formerly from the city, recently built a small kennel to accommodate about a dozen dogs. The kennels are sparkling clean, well-ventilated in summer, and heated in winter. The owner has a nice way with the animals, and at three dollars a day, or twenty dollars a week per head, manages to make a fairly decent sum without a tremendous amount of work. One thing that he does that we particularly like, is to remember to tell dog owners to be sure and bring along the dog's favorite toys and blanket—if the dog, like Linus, is partial to one. This seems to help a lot in making the dogs feel at home.

Whichever auxiliary method you choose to help bring in money, you will probably still be very much involved with your garden—if you find that you like gardening and can make things grow—you will no doubt have surplus fruits and vegetables which you can sell. Once you are established and known in an area, you can get people to come to you for their fresh produce needs. Advertising in the local papers is helpful, and, if you are near a well-traveled road, so is a sign at the entrance to your property to attract passing motorists. If you are in resort or vacation country, you will probably attract weekenders going back to the city, in addition to those summer people (and year 'rounders, too) who don't have the time or perhaps the inclination to put in gardens of their own. All are eager customers for homegrown produce and—as you probably know from your own excursions into the country—like nothing better than loading themselves down with just-picked corn, fresh tomatoes, beans, summer squash, and other garden delectables. The same holds true for cut flowers, especially if they are made into attractive arrangements. Some people like to leave standing orders for special occasions or for weekly arrangements of seasonal flowers, often bringing their own favorite vases and bowls.

Local inns, motels, and resorts can be contacted, too, and perhaps signed up for regular delivery of flower arrangements, vegetables, and special fruits or berries. Small, independent grocery and general stores can also be contacted. If you are suddenly overwhelmed with the bounty from your garden—and after canning and freezing for your own family's winter needs and selling to all your local outlets, you still have stuff to sell—you can always pile your car or station wagon with produce and get out and peddle! If there are concentrations of summer cottages anywhere around, you'll be surprised at how well you will do—and meet a lot of new people besides.

In the autumn and at various holiday times—Halloween, Thanksgiving, Christmas—dried flower arrangements or combinations of flowers and harvest fruits and vegetables have a good sales potential. Wild grasses and many dried weeds can also be made into charming and decorative compositions. If you find that you really have a knack for this sort of thing, you can make Christmas wreaths, door, window, and mantle decorations from natural things gathered from your fields, woods, and garden. Such materials as pine cones—from the tiniest to gigantic—dried flower pods, dried artichokes, nuts, berries, and wild things native to your particular region can be combined into original and unique ornamentations. Your customers could be gift shops, local garden centers and nurseries, health food and crafts shops. As you become better known, customers may deal directly with you at your own place. You can get pointers on drying flowers and other vegetation from your Cooperative Extension Service, your local library, and back issues of magazines such as *Woman's Day*, which feature such do-it-yourself projects in holiday issues.

Only you can decide whether you will want to garden organically. Organic foods are tremendously popular right now—especially with the ecology-minded. Our guess is that they will increase in popularity, as more and more people experiment with organic methods and become more familiar—and successful—with ways of controlling insects and plant diseases by natural means. Prices for organically-grown foods are higher than for those grown with chemicals, but there seems to be a ready market for them. There is a growing movement among organic farmers at the present time to establish some form of nationally recognized certification for those who market organic foods, so that the consumer will know that the claim "organically grown" is true. Only those who meet certain standards will be allowed the certification.

Robert Rodale, son of J. I. Rodale, the granddaddy of organic gardening, is spearheading the movement for certification, and the Rodale Press is now granting such certification to some eighty farms that meet its standards. By the time this book is in print, this number will no doubt have increased considerably. But if you do go in for organic gardening, you will want to know more about it. You can write the Rodale Press, Inc., Emmaus, Pennsylvania 18049 for information. You should also subscribe to the Rodale Press magazine, *Organic Gardening*, and by all means buy the *Encyclopedia of Organic Gardening*, by J. I. Rodale, at your bookstore or from Rodale Press.

chapter 6

GETTING TO KNOW
THE TERRITORY

Once you've settled enough so that the house is in minimal
running order and you're fairly comfortable, take a little
breathing spell, get out of the house, and introduce yourself to some of the local customs and people. You can be
quite sure that the fact that you are there is known to far
more people than you imagine—and there has probably
been considerable speculation as to what the people who
bought the old Caruthers' place (that's you) are like.

If there is a general store nearby, or a little local grocery
store, go down, buy a few things, and introduce yourself.
They'll be glad to meet you and probably very pleased to
answer any questions you may have about almost anything. These little stores are veritable gold mines of information, and the people who run them know about everything that is happening or about to happen in the area. If
you need some specialized help, such as the name of a
good plumber, where to buy firewood, or whatever, they
can probably tell you. The plumber might be the owner's
father-in-law, and his cousin Joe might turn out to be the
only mason within fifty miles. Many country stores also
have bulletin boards, and the notices make for excellent
reading. "Ironing done at home—snow-white kittens for
free—1963 Plymouth for sale. $100. Runs good.—Dining
room set, six chairs, only $25—Car pool to Springfield,
call evenings." You, too, can post your wants and, who

knows, might find exactly what you are looking for, or just the person to buy what *you* have for sale.

These little country grocery stores are often Mom and Pop operations, and the people work very hard—especially if the store is in or near a resort area. In addition to groceries, and sometimes meat, they carry a few patent medicines, a little stationery, candles, and odds and ends of almost anything else you're likely to run out of. They are often the only local place where you can get newspapers and magazines, and are likely to stay open at least six-and-a-half days a week. If you want a daily paper, a weekly, or the Sunday edition of a Big City paper, let them know, and they will reserve your copy for you. It's funny how much at home you feel, almost immediately, when you go down to get *your* paper and it's got *your* name on it. Suddenly, you're part of the community!

Small stores, of course, can't compete with the big supermarkets on a price basis, so things are apt to be a bit more expensive, but the owners try to make up for this with service and the convenience of being right on the spot. Once they know you, they'll cash checks for you and even extend credit, but it's usually a good idea to establish yourself first on a cash basis before asking for it. If you do eventually establish credit, make a special point of paying *that* bill promptly. Actually, all your local bills should be paid promptly. One reason is that small tradespeople have to pay their own bills in order to stay in business, and they don't usually have a large amount of capital behind them (although sometimes the grocer and the liquor dealer are more affluent than anyone else in town, including you). The other, and less altruistic reason is that if you *don't* pay promptly, everybody and his brother is going to know about it. This is just one more black mark against the city—and city people, and ex-city people—who are now country people.

For reasons of economy, you'll probably want to make a weekly shopping expedition to the nearest big shopping center for staples, canned goods, and so on. If you want to be able to pay by check, you'll no doubt have to fill out some form of credit questionnaire, which can be a bit sticky if you are self-employed or not yet established in some kind of job or business endeavor. As we mentioned earlier in another chapter, it's a good idea to make arrangements of this sort *before* you quit your job, if you possibly can. There doesn't seem to be much of a problem about a store's accepting an out-of-town or out-of-state check if they can check your credit or your credentials and they look good. In resort areas, of course, they do this all the time with summer people or ski people or whatever.

Once you're living in an area all the time, however, it is a good idea to have a local bank account. You don't have to keep your entire fortune in it—just enough to meet the bank's minimum account requirements and establish yourself as a citizen in good standing. When you open the account, try to meet the head man, if you can. Local bankers are—because it's their business—very knowledgeable about what's going on in the area and can be helpful in many ways. If you are thinking of starting your own business, want a loan, or want to take out a mortgage, your local banker is an essential man to know. Small-town banks are awfully nice about honoring your checks, too, if you are a depositor and happen to overdraw your account either through error or a deposited check not clearing as fast as you thought. They will usually send you a polite little notice to that effect, but unlike a big city bank, they seldom bounce your checks unless you take advantage of their forebearance and make a habit of overdrawing.

Just as in the city, you'll probably have to shop around a bit before you can find the places where you can get just the kind of meat you want, the right cheeses, good crusty bread and so on. And in some areas, you never will. You'll either have to order from the city, learn to like the local provender, or make or grow whatever it is yourself. We spent several months trying to find a good meat market because we didn't like the meat at the supermarket in the next town. If we were invited out for dinner, the first thing we'd do if we liked what was served would be to ask the hostess or host where they got their meat. We got some good leads and a few bum steers (now, *that's* a pun!). We finally ended up by getting excellent beef at the local grocery down in the village, veal in a neighboring town across the river, and the greatest smoked ham ever at Bury's Market, up Moodus-way—about a three-mile drive and worth every mile of it. They also smoke their own bacon, and make their own sausage, in addition to the family-held recipe for smoking ham. Their chickens are good, too, and they carry a fine Vermont cheddar, some good Danish blue cheese, and country eggs. All in all, a most fortunate discovery that we learned about by asking friends. Seafood, though, is another matter, and only available fresh by driving about fifteen miles down to the shore, except in May, when the local shad run just a stone's throw away. Happily, even though the river is polluted, it doesn't seem to have affected the shad, which is delicious. At least, it has been up until now—and various local and state groups are trying to clean up the river. "They" say that maybe in five years we can even swim in it!

Check around, too, for local fruit orchards and farms where you can get fresh garden produce in season. Even if you grow your own, you probably won't have everything —especially in the beginning.

As we mentioned in Chapter Two, local papers are a big help in getting to know the territory, as are local Yellow Pages. However, in certain rural areas, the pickin's can be pretty slim in the Yellows, because there just aren't that many concerns around, except maybe fifty miles away. Most local newspapers do have a Business Service Directory, or some similar category, and here is where you'll find the plumber's advertisement, the electrician's advertisement, the road man, the well-drilling outfit, and so on. Ask around about these fellows before you engage their services. They'll probably be known by name, anyway, and while it's unlikely that a local tradesperson would bad-mouth another (especially to a newcomer) you may be able to tell from their reactions in other ways how they feel about the quality of service offered. Sometimes they might just pass the matter off by saying they don't know anything about it, another time it might be, "Yep, Joe's good and so's Jack—and then, of course, there's Jim" and so on. Then it's really up to you to make the decision, or continue to pursue the matter until you finally feel you've got a reading. The other way—less cautious but more direct—is just to call the fellow, and have him come over and give you an estimate on whatever it is you want done.

There may come a time when you will need one of these essential service people in a hurry, so even if you don't have any major work to be done right away, it's a good idea to make the initial contact when the need may not be so acute. The plumbing system, for instance, may be run-ning pretty well now, but there's no harm in asking the plumber to check it out and perhaps explain any part of the system that is not familar to you. If you've bought an older house, you will no doubt eventually want to replace some of the fixtures and probably replace some of the old iron pipe with copper or one of the newer plastic pipes. If the plumber has been in the community for a long time, he'll probably know all about the peculiarities of the sys-tem, so you might as well find out about them sooner than later and get to know each other at the same time.

If you haven't already checked out the wiring in the house before you moved in, it's important that you have a licensed electrician go over the system as soon as possible —certainly before you bring any additional appliances, such as a washing machine, dishwasher, blender, etc. Older houses may only be able to handle 120 volts, and you'll have to have 240 volts for more modern conven-iences. Also, you may have to replace some of the old wiring.

Another fellow you may need in a hurry is your oil-burner serviceman or other heating serviceman. Have your heating system checked out as soon as you move in, even if it's midsummer. All systems burning fossil fuels should be cleaned at least once a year, anyway, and summer is actually the best time to do it, because the service people aren't so busy. Usually the people from whom you buy your fuel are the best bet for repairs and servicing. It's to their advantage to keep the burner burning, and you warm and cozy.

Before we get too far from the subject of the local papers, let us remind you again about the classified ads. If you haven't been a "classified" fan before, you'll really be surprised at how much useful information you can pick up. You'll learn about household goods for sale, nearby auctions and barn sales, handymen, babysitters, and maybe even a lady who will give you a hand with the housework from time to time. Under General and Private Instructions, you might find that you can take a beginner's sewing course not too far away, or learn to play South Indian music for $5.00 an hour. While you're doing this not unpleasant research work, you might as well start a card file on some of the vital statistics you pick up, so that even if you don't need any of these services or people right now, you'll have the information when you do. Most companies or business services advertise on a fairly regular basis, but individuals are apt to get discouraged or run out of money and advertise just the one time.

Finding The Right Doctor: Just as other systems need checkups and repairs, so do our own systems from time to time. When you move into a new community, it is very important to line up a good doctor as soon as possible—*before* you have an emergency—not during. This is especially true if you have a chronic or recurrent physical problem.

In your search for the right doctor for your family, start

first with your friends and neighbors. In rural or semirural areas, there probably won't be all that many doctors to choose from, so when you get a few names, go to the nearest library and check out their qualifications in the *Directory of Medical Specialists*. Many internists today practice general medicine, and in the directory you'll find out where they went to medical school, where they interned, and when.

If the doctor is a specialist in any particular branch of medicine, this too will be noted, as will his certification by the supervising Board in his field. Certification means that he has had several years as a resident physician in his specialty—after his internship—and that he has passed stiff examinations—oral, written, and practical. If he is listed as "Board-eligible" he has put in his residency time but, for whatever reason, has not passed the Board exams. This does not necessarily mean he is not a competent doctor— some people are good at taking exams and some just aren't. Even the specialist who is certified, once he has that stamp of approval, may continue practicing his speciality just as he learned it forty years ago. Despite pressure from many in the medical field, there are, as yet, no mandatory requirements that he continue his education and keep abreast of new developments in his field, although many doctors feel that within a few years, periodic reexaminations will be automatic. If there is not a *Directory of Medical Specialists* in your library, or no library, check with the administrator of your nearest community hospital and ask for the names of GP's or internists in the area.

You probably already know whether there are hospitals in your community or in the surrounding area. If they are teaching hospitals connected with a medical school or college you are in luck, because teaching hospitals usually have fine doctors on their staffs, including specialists. There are many excellent community hospitals, too, and if you have occasion to go to one, you will find them generally pleasant, and well administered, with a friendly atmosphere, quite different from the Big-City hospitals, which are often understaffed, cold, and impersonal. In order to keep their accreditation, all such hospitals must keep to certain high standards, and if your doctor is affiliated with the local community hospital, he too, must practice quality medicine in order to retain his privileges at the hospital.

Country doctors are, of necessity, usually general practitioners and are used to treating everything from sprained backs to strained marriages. The Good Old Country Doc of fiction and film, racing through the snowy night in his buggy or 1925 Buick to deliver his eighth baby of the day, is no longer with us, except in rare instances. While some doctors do still make house calls, most prefer to see patients in their offices, so when you have found the name of a doctor who seems as though he'd be right for you, make an appointment with him and go up and introduce yourself; tell him where you live, how many in your family, and so on. Doing this *before* anyone gets sick, gives you a feeling of real confidence—especially if you happen to like each other.

Another way to find a doctor, of course, is just to look in the Yellow Pages of your telephone directory—and you might have to do this in a real emergency—but it's chancy. Doctors are only obligated to attend those patients they have seen before, so if the doctor happens to be busy or just doesn't want to see you, you're out of luck. Your only recourse in that case is to call the State Police, and indeed, you might be better off to do this than to chance the trial-and-error method.

Finding a good dentist is not always easy, and if you had a dentist you liked before you moved, it would be a good idea to ask him if he could recommend someone in the area. Your new doctor can probably refer you to someone, too, or you can check with your community hospital or with a dental college affiliated with a local university or teaching hospital. A lot of people, however, become so attached to one dentist that they will travel halfway across the world rather than go to a strange dentist. If you're like that, you're destined to make the trip back to the Big City whenever you have need of dental services.

There are so many competent dentists today, and so many new developments in the field, that, except in certain special situations, you will undoubtedly find—especially among younger dentists—just the right man for the whole family.

chapter 7
MAKING FRIENDS

You can expect to feel a bit lonely when you first move to the country, but probably no more so than if you moved to a strange city or suburb. If you're way out in back country, though, you'll certainly notice the lack of people —not friends—just the many people you are accustomed to having around in the city. It may take you a little while to adjust to their absence, but it's rather a pleasant experience.

While you're busy getting settled you probably won't have time to do any socializing, but it's a good idea to establish communications with your nearest neighbors. Maybe they'll drop over to say hello or even bring a freshly baked pie or cake to welcome you, but if they don't, don't be hurt. Without being pushy, take the initiative yourself. Give them a call and introduce yourself, or if you see them outside the house, stop by. Chances are, unless they happen to be odd folk indeed, that they'll be friendly and will probably already know your name and a little about you, because the arrival of a new neighbor in the country is an event. You may be living near each other for a long time, and in an emergency, your neighbor is the first person you turn to. You can usually assume that they are going to be as anxious to like you as you are to like them, and when you first meet, each of you will probably be as curious and hopeful as the other.

You may have people from all kinds of different backgrounds as neighbors, and with all kinds of different interests. The one across the road may be very rich and the one on your side, very poor. In one relatively small section, you may find a farmer, an artist, a factory worker, or a retired investment banker. Not much in common on the surface, except that they happen to be neighbors, but often that's enough to create a friendly bond.

Establish friendly relationships, if you can, but don't become too intimate, too soon. Friendship can be a very fragile thing at times, and good neighbors are too valuable to risk by becoming too chummy.

You'll learn a lot from your neighbors, especially if they are old timers. If you ask questions, they'll probably tell you more about your house and what's wrong with it than you'll want to know. They can also start your general education in the community—the problems, the personalities, and the relationship of each to the other.

You'll find that if you can take a more or less relaxed attitude about making friends, you'll be more successful. You may be used to doing things in a hurry in the city, but friendships anywhere—except the most superficial ones—take time to develop and to ripen. If you come on too crisp, too brusque, too demanding, you'll just put people off. Some people say that it's hard to make friends in the country—maybe that's the reason. Country people are generally very friendly, but they can be quite cautious about establishing new friendships. There isn't that immediate informality that you find so often in the city or the suburbs, where people call each other by their first names right away. Sometimes people who have known and liked each other for years are still "Mr. Jones" or "Mrs. Jones". A bit stiff, perhaps, but if you think of it as being naturally a bit more reserved, and follow the local customs, you'll get along just fine.

Sometimes one hears newcomers to a community complain that there are "none of our kind of people around" or "there just aren't any interesting people in this place." And indeed, you may at times feel this way. But usually, "your" kind of people are to be found doing the kinds of things you like to do. If you like to paint, sculpt, or weave—look for groups who are engaged in these things. Take courses in arts and crafts. If there are no such activities in your community, perhaps there may be in an adjoining one. And if you can't find any at all, organize a group yourself. If it's music, theatre, dance, or any of the other lively arts, do the same. You may be just the catalyst the community was waiting for, and you might suddenly have more friends than you know what to do with.

You may also meet people with whom you have common interests by joining the local horticultural or garden club, historical society, conservation and ecology group, mental health association, or political club. Or it might be the Chamber of Commerce, the Lion's Club, Rotary Club, or other fraternal organization. Church is another good way to get to know people. A country church can be a pretty active institution, with lots of events scheduled, and all sorts of smaller groups within the church. Even if you don't belong to a church, it's nice to get over for special fund-raising events—not only to meet people and perhaps sample the suppers and baked goods for sale—but to show your goodwill and interest in the community.

You can find out about what's happening in the area by reading your local papers, keeping an eye on local bulletin boards in stores or at the Town Hall. Your local librarian is often a good person to chat with about various cultural activities, and if you have children in school, you will hear about all sorts of occasions and festivities where you might lend a hand.

There may be a group of unregenerate city people in your town, and you may be tempted to become involved. These are people who have moved to the country, but only in body. Their spirits and minds are still in the city, and they care neither for country people nor country ways. They complain about almost everything. "You can't get a decent meal in any of the local restaurants"—the "locals" are lazy, inefficient, sometimes downright dishonest—and so on. This is a good group to avoid, because aside from the fact that they will give you a lot of incorrect and probably biased information, their carping will detract considerably from the pleasure you take in country living.

It probably will be a year or so before you will begin to feel that you have any really close friends—maybe not even then. But even this is better than those quick intimacies where—after a few months—the bloom is gone, and you are either stuck with a relationship you wish would go away, or have to try to cool it, which isn't easy without hurting feelings.

You may not even want close friends, or not right now. And the nice thing about most country people that we know is that they do understand the desire on the part of others just to be left alone. As long as you're friendly, not too distant, and don't act superior, it's fine with them. Some people up the road from us who have owned their house for three or four years now, can only get up weekends and for an occasional week or two. When they do come, they just want to enjoy relaxing in the country to the maximum, so they don't mix much with their neighbors and don't go to parties or meetings, and everyone understands why and that's that. Maybe someday they will want to be more social, and that will be fine too. So if you have work to do, or for whatever reason, want to maintain your privacy, just let enough of the reason be known so that you'll not be considered a snob. If you do take this road, however, don't forget to donate to important community causes when approached, so that you won't be altogether forgotten. If that happened, then you might be the one with hurt feelings.

Social customs differ a little in the country in another rather nice way. If people invite you over for dinner or a party, they don't necessarily assume that you're going to invite them right back—especially if you're trying to get your house fixed up. Eventually, though, they'll want to come over and see what you've done to the old place; so when you're ready, it's a nice idea to have a little gathering, even if it takes a bit of an effort.

As for what to wear when invited out in the country—a pretty good rule of thumb is to wear casual clothes if you're going to a city person's house, but dress up a little if you're going to a country person's home, unless it's a barbeque or some other outside activity. If in doubt, you can always check, just like in the city.

chapter 8
RAISING CHILDREN IN THE COUNTRY

In the not so distant past it was common practice for city people who moved to the country to look down their noses at the local public schools and to send their children away to private schools where they could get a better and "more rounded" education and be with children of social backgrounds similar to their own. Sometimes the children were also sent away to camp in the summer, where recreation would be planned and supervised. While the parents thought they were doing the best thing for the child, the cost to the child was often high. Because the child was seldom at home except during holidays, he or she never really had an opportunity to feel part of the community or accepted by it. Also they missed a lot of the joys of growing up in the country—the opportunity to have a garden, a pet goat or other animal, raise rabbits or chickens, or any of the hundreds of things that country kids can do, including just "messing around" on a lazy summer day with some pals. They also missed the companionship of their parents.

Today, more and more families, especially young parents who leave the city looking for a better way of life for themselves and their children, are doing the natural thing —keeping their children at home and allowing them to go to school and grow up in the community. The parents' values have changed, and it no longer seems vital that their children wear the "old school tie" or go to a school that will almost guarantee their getting into the "right" college.

College admissions requirements are also considerably different than they were even five years ago. There is far less emphasis on grades and social background and far more on the type of mind the young person has; his or her interests and potential for learning. Also, a great many young people who would automatically have been "college material" a few years ago, no longer feel that they wish or need four years of higher education. Many are settling for the two-year community colleges or none at all—preferring to have some experience in the "real world" before they decide on their life style.

Many of these young people, including some who have already graduated from college, are turning their backs on conventional careers of the past and turning to those things they can do with their hands, bodies, and hearts, as well as with their minds. Vocational training or learning a trade is no longer just for those not smart enough to make it in an office. Craftsmanship, artisanship, and pride and pleasure in the actual performance of the work itself, are values once again taking their rightful place in our society, just as they were valued when this country was first settled. The child who is raised in the country is a fortunate child, because he or she can learn these values firsthand.

The quality of the schools in any community depends to a large degree on the kind of people who live in the community, their income level, and the kind of education they want for their children. Obviously, in communities where a majority of parents have college backgrounds, more will be demanded of the school system than if the parents have only grade school and some high school education. If yours is a growing community, attracting new people and new enterprises, there will be an infusion of fresh blood and fresh ideas into the entire area and into what may have been a static, or under-stimulated and under-financed school system. These new people will also, of course, bring new money into the community, a good deal of which, in the form of taxes, will eventually go into improving the schools. And if present proposals are voted into law, money from the federal government will also begin to go into schools. At the present time, however, many rural and semirural schools, just like city schools, are experiencing growing pains—especially those in communities where rapid growth is taking place. Some of the problems in these communities are too many children and not enough space, too little funding for either new or enlarged schools, and not enough new teachers to handle the increased number of children.

You may encounter these problems to a greater or lesser degree, depending on the community into which you have moved. And you may find yourself far more involved in the schools than you were in the city. Presumably, if you have school-age children, you will have checked into the quality of the schools before you made the move, so you will have some idea of what to expect and some idea of whether, and to what extent, you will have to augment at home what your child is learning at school. A lot depends on the individual teacher who is assigned to your child's class and on how he or she and your child get along. Some children can't cope when too many demands are made of them. Some are so responsive to what is being taught that there is no need to make demands. Others need teachers who do make demands on them, and only feel a sense of accomplishment when they are able to meet these demands. You may find wonderful, dedicated teachers in the most unlikely rural or semirural areas, and you may find just the opposite. You may find schools that have excellent music, art, and drama programs—in addition to the 3R's—and teachers who are interested enough in their young pupils to organize all sorts of field trips to points of interest in the area. On the other hand, some teachers are only interested in getting the day's work done as quickly as possible and in a most routine manner.

If you find that there are a lot of gaps in the curriculum, you will no doubt want to try to fill as many as you can while, at the same time, working to improve the school. One way is to organize some field trips of your own, especially if the schools don't go in for this sort of thing. Besides, part of the fun of living in the country, for both you and your children, is exploring and finding things together. There will probably be many interesting places you can visit: farms, lumber mills, certain plants and factories that have visitors' days, nearby museums and—especially interesting to children—any place where there is Indian lore. If you live near coastal areas, there may be seaports and marine museums, sailing ships, and other relics of bygone days. In several sections of the country there are railroad museums, where old steam engines still chug and puff to the delight of the small fry. And, of course, there are various state and national parks with camping grounds, picnic areas, and so forth.

There may be other educational and cultural gaps you will want to fill from time to time, especially with older children, by taking them (and sometimes their friends, too) to concerts, plays, art exhibits, and museums in the metropolitan center that is nearest you.

This sort of excursion, of course, was much easier when you lived in the city and, because of distances in the country, you may have to make a real effort to initiate them, but if they are important to you, you will. You'll probably also enjoy them yourself.

You may find, too, that there is a lot more going on in your own bailiwick than you had at first realized. In the summer and fall, especially, there are all kinds of cultural and artistic happenings in many rural areas. Arts and crafts shows, historical celebrations, harvest festivities, and music and drama festivals—in addition to such not-so-cultural but fun and appetite-pleasing occasions as strawberry festivals, outdoor barbeques, clambakes, chicken-bakes, cake sales, and political picnics. We have many activities of this sort in our area, including the very special Moodus Drum and Fife Corps—a group of involved and talented citizen-musicians, ranging in age from about ten or eleven to sixty or more. Dressed in colorful Revolutionary costumes, various drum and fife corps bands from Maine to Virginia meet in different communities for their Annual Musters. And if your patriotic fervor is simmering down and your blood is in need of a little stirring up, all you need to completely revitalize both, is to attend one of these enchanting but ear-numbing events.

And then, of course, there are the annual county and state fairs—just like in the movies. A real gala, complete with horse and oxen pulls, blue ribbons to young and old for the best of breed, whether it is a pig, the most elegant steer, the best milk cow, the biggest pumpkin, or the finest ear of corn. There will also be prizes for the clearest jellies, most tasty preserves, most succulent pickles. In addition, there are arts and crafts exhibits, flower shows, target shooting, rodeos, cotton candy, and everything else that goes to make for a great day at the fair.

When spring arrives, you and your children will be eager to start the garden. Most children are enthralled and fascinated by the process of growth, and younger children will particularly enjoy having their own little garden, perhaps alongside the family vegetable plot. From the time the first seeds go in the ground until the plants reach maturity and are ready for picking, the child will take a great deal of personal pride in "his" or "her" accomplishment, especially when the results reach the family dinner table. Older children also usually enjoy gardening and can be a big help in this and other family projects. Most country children are assigned chores around the house and grounds as their special responsibility, including helping with the care of any animals the family may have.

Your children, too, will be able to shoulder considerable

responsibility as they grow accustomed to country life. If you have several children, it's a good idea to rotate chores so that each one has a chance to do a little of everything and none feels that he or she is getting the short end of the stick.

Your children will, of course, make friends in school, but once the school bus has dropped them off for the day, they may be somewhat at loose ends unless you are fortunate enough to have neighbors with children around their age. They may be somewhat lonely in the beginning, so it's a good idea to get them involved in projects of their own, along with helping out on family projects, whether it's baking bread, digging a trench, painting the barn, or whatever else needs to be done. There are all kinds of special projects that country kids get a kick out of, including raising rabbits, squabs, or bantam chickens for sale. Waiting for the baby rabbits and watching for the baby chicks to break through the shells are high events in a child's life. Laying hens, too, make an excellent project and turn every day into an Easter egg hunt. And, of course, they will want to have a dog now that they are in the country, and it probably won't be long before there's at least one kitten on the place.

Older children in the country also keep pretty busy making money. In most communities, there is plenty of demand for kids to help others with yard work, housework, light carpentry, cleaning basements and attics, shoveling snow and mowing lawns, and, of course, baby-sitting.

Parents hiring kids to baby-sit are usually quite willing to pick up the sitter and bring him or her home, but when hiring out for other jobs, the kids are more or less expected to bring themselves. Unless they can walk or have a bike (or until they have saved up enough and are old enough to buy a car) this leaves you as chauffeur—which can take up a good deal of your time, not to mention mileage. The best thing to do is to get them bikes as soon as you possibly can. This not only frees you but also gives them a sense of freedom.

Your children may also be interested in becoming Cub Scouts or Brownies, and when they reach age twelve, Boy Scouts or Girl Scouts. Most people are fairly familiar with these organizations, which operate in both city and country, and hundreds of thousands of boys and girls over the years have benefited tremendously from being members. Another organization with which you may or may not be familiar is the National 4-H Club. The 4-H's stand for Head, Heart, Hands, and Health, and the program is designed to help and encourage boys and girls from nine to nineteen years of age to "learn by doing" in coping with the situations in which they find themselves in the world today, whether on the farm, at home, or in urban or suburban areas. The program is a part of the national educational system of Cooperative Extension work. The United States Department of Agriculture provides national leadership, and the state extension services provide state leadership to the program. Through individual 4-H Clubs, each with its own volunteer leader, young people can gain any number of skills, make new friends, and have a lot of fun by participating in the various projects. They can learn all about electricity, how to use tools, how to sew, cook, bake, preserve food, make candles, take care of their bicycles, do woodworking and other crafts. Those in rural areas can also learn about livestock, dairy and beef cattle, horses, goats, sheep, swine, etc. and how to breed them, show them, and judge them. In addition, 4-H Clubs offer all kinds of natural science projects—such as exploring the world of plants and soils, forestry projects, how to collect, preserve, and identify insects—along with a lot of other fascinating things concerning the world around us. Club members can even learn public speaking, newspaper writing, and parliamentary procedure. Leaders of the projects are parents, college students, older teens, and other adults who like to work with young people. To find out more about 4-H Clubs in your area, contact your County Agent at the local Cooperative Extension Service. You'll be glad you did.

Regardless of whether your children become involved with 4-H, you will definitely want to contact your County Agent on your own, because his help and assistance, and the numerous publications available through the Extension Service, will be invaluable to you, as we discuss elsewhere in this book.

You will still, however, want to refer to various outside publications and books from a public library, and you and your children will be fortunate indeed, if there is a good one not too far away—preferably one your children can walk or bike to. Even today, not all rural areas have access to a public library, despite the fact that librarians are working hard to achieve this goal. A plan is now in operation in about twelve states that uses a community library as the basic unit from which—through an inter-library loan network reaching to the county, regional, state, and even national libraries—all kinds of books, pamphlets, magazines, and reference materials are made available, even to very remote rural areas. The plan, called Library Systems Development, also makes available many visual and audio educational aids to local groups of adults who may use the community library as a meeting place, making use of these facilities. There is also Bookmobile Service in many remote areas where the arrival of this little traveling library is eagerly awaited by both adults and children.

A good reference library at home is desirable, too, and we suggest having the best one you can afford. Not only will the children find it a big help in doing homework and their various projects, but so will the rest of the family.

chapter 9
BECOMING PART OF
THE COMMUNITY

One of the reasons cited by many former city dwellers for moving to a smaller community is the feeling of personal effectiveness in community affairs. And only someone who knows the frustrations of being a very small frog in a very big city pond can appreciate the contrast. Even if you haven't been much of a joiner before, you will probably find certain organizations or group activities in which you will want to participate. Unless you are in a very rural area where there will not be much going on, once your presence is known to the community, you will probably be invited to join a lot of things. And unless you have an awfully good excuse, you will be hard pressed to refuse at least one or two of these invitations. If you are really serious about wanting to put down roots in a community, this is about the best way to let that be known.

What to become involved in depends, of course, on your own interests, the kind of community you are living in, the community needs, and how much time and energy you can afford to give. If your children are in the local schools, you will be drawn into the PTA and other school activities and will have the opportunity to meet people right away and find out a lot about community problems and what's going on. If you don't have children in the schools, you may have to scratch around a bit before you know what's happening and which organizations you might want to participate in: community fund raising, environmental and conservation, church, cultural, educational, fraternal, business, political, or purely social and recreational.

It's a good idea, at first, to be a little cautious and not get involved in too much, too soon. Certainly not until you know exactly what the organizations stand for, and until you've had a chance to make sure that this is a group you want to join. As a newcomer you will probably be attracted to others in the same boat, especially if your interests are similar. But in order to avoid any feeling on the part of the townspeople that "the city people all stick together," it might also behoove you to participate in at least one of the older, more established groups—especially if the community as a whole stands to benefit by whatever the organization is doing.

You will, of course, want to make a donation (it doesn't have to be large) to such local community services as the town ambulance service and the volunteer fire department. We have a special admiration for our own town fire fighters. An all-volunteer group, they really lay it on the line for the community—getting up at all hours of the night in all kinds of weather, dropping whatever they are doing during the day whenever the fire siren sounds. Last year, we had occasion to see them operate when our neighbor's house caught on fire. They came quickly and were as efficient and professional as all get out. If they hadn't been, the large Victorian frame structure would have been completely consumed. But because they got there in a hurry, and knew exactly what to do, they managed to keep the fire confined to just one room.

If you plan to go into business in the community, to hang out your shingle, or to open a shop or store, you will almost certainly be invited to become a member of the Chamber of Commerce. This will give you a chance to meet business and professional people you may not have met before, plus the opportunity to learn more about the town from the inside. Chamber of Commerce people are usually boosters, sometimes boasters, and frequently the "movers"—those who want to encourage new business and industry to come in, and who are in favor of "growth" in general. You may find yourself in agreement with some of their objectives and completely opposed to others. But if the success or failure of your own business depends on the cooperation and goodwill of the town, you will probably be well advised to join. Also, your own words will carry more weight as a member of the group than as an outsider.

As soon as you have established the local residence requirement, you will want to register, so that you can vote when the time comes. If you want to be able to vote in the primaries, you will, of course, have to be a registered member of one of the political parties. If you really want to be a part of the action, you should attend party caucuses, and, after you get the lay of the land, put your own name in nomination for election or political appointment.

As a property owner and a resident of the community, you will, naturally, want to have your say in whatever matters are up for discussion at town or community meetings, and at public hearings. These meetings are the democratic process at work, and often "the wheels grind exceeding slow." You may be accustomed to doing things in a hurry, and, indeed, it is sometimes difficult not to become impatient while each person has his or her say, especially if the matter at hand is something with which you may have had previous experience. The answers may be piercingly clear to you, but it pays to bide your time, and when you do get up to have *your* say, not to talk down to the local citizenry. They are often just as much aware of the shortcomings of their community as you are but don't appreciate being told what's wrong by outsiders, or how it is done in the Big City. Schools, especially, are a sore point in small communities. They take a big chunk out of the taxpayer's dollar, and school budgets are painstakingly scrutinized before being approved. One way to get everybody's back up at such meetings is for you, the newcomer, to come on as Grand Instructor to the entire town.

Another sensitive point with many rural Americans is the idea that anyone has a right to tell them what they can or cannot do with their land. Farm families, especially, still cling to the attitudes of an earlier America, when a man's home was his castle and a man's land his fief-dom—to hold forever to himself and his heirs or to dispose of as he sees fit, to anyone he pleases for whatever purpose the buyer chooses. The concept of *land use*—where, after study and evaluation by local, county, and sometimes state authorities, restrictions are placed on the use of land so that it can only be used in ways which the commission or board feels would be nondetrimental to the locality and environment as a whole—is a foreign one and still highly controversial in thousands of small towns and rural communities.

In some communities there is even strong opposition to simple zoning ordinances which designate certain areas for business and industrial use and others as residential and commercial districts. Frequently, one town will adopt zoning ordinances while an adjoining sister town or village will not. It is not difficult to tell which is which, with roads in the unzoned countryside a hodgepodge of filling stations, blatantly designed eateries, drive-ins, billboards, poorly situated industrial plants, and all the rest of the all-too-familiar signs of visual pollution and creeping urbanization. Yet there are still those who want no part of planning of any sort, and when the subject of zoning or land-use planning comes up at a town meeting or public hearing, the fireworks start.

One group may be against setting up a Planning and Zoning Board because they want to attract industry or business to the community and want no restrictions as to where the companies can build. Another group might be speculating in land, seeing in the natural beauty of the area opportunities for vacation houses or recreational developments. Still another group may be against anything that would impede the path of "progress" as they see it. Often lined up with these special interest groups are the Old Timers who are against planning and zoning simply because they regard it as an infringement on their personal liberties.

If you are fortunate enough to have settled in a community where this and similar battles have already been fought—and, we hope, won—you will probably want to turn your attention to other matters. But if the battle has not yet begun, or is still raging (and it looks as if it will be raging all through the seventies), you will want to be involved in it—not only to protect your own property against the encroachment of unplanned and uncontrolled growth (and the environmental blight that follows it), but to save open space for the benefit of all and protect the character of the community and countryside that attracted you in the first place.

As a newcomer, you will be somewhat at a disadvantage until you learn what's what and who's who, and what it is all about; and your support may be solicited by people representing many divergent points of view. You'll be well advised not to align yourself with any particular segment of the community until you are absolutely sure that their aims coincide with yours and that you are not getting into a select group whose main concern is their own special interest rather than the welfare and well-being of the community as a whole. But when you are sure—jump in with both feet.

In order for any community to survive, there must be some way for the people in it to make a living. As a member of the community, you will begin to appreciate its problems from the inside, especially if you, too, are dependent for your daily bread on the economic health of the general area. In small cities, towns, and rural areas all over the country, the problem is how to preserve the attractiveness and character of the area while at the same time planning for and making room for the development necessary for economic survival. This is when land-use planning is of the highest importance, and where you will want to join other informed and concerned citizens in working with community leaders, public officials, and—more and more often—specialists from nearby colleges and universities in supporting and working for a quality environment. After all, this is really what you came for, isn't it?

If you do find yourself involved in a planning and open-space conservation struggle between various factions in your new town and want to know how to go about winning the battle to save open space and/or setting up a land trust, you will find a book called *Property Power* by Mary Anne Guitar (Doubleday, $6.95) of enormous help. Running on an environmental platform. Ms. Guitar was the first woman to be elected to her town's (Redding, Connecticut) Board of Selectmen and was a leading activist in organizing the townsfolk to set aside a large and environmentally valuable piece of property as a land trust for the benefit of the entire town. Her book recounts the action, tells why it was important, and lays down guidelines for similar successful endeavors in all parts of the nation.

chapter 10
GETTING ALONG WITH
THE LOCAL POPULACE

How much you will enjoy living in the country and how much you gain from the experience each day will depend, among other things, on your desire and ability to establish good relationships, not only with your neighbors but with the community in general. There are some city people who move to the country and never bother to get to know the local people at all, except in a most superficial manner. This is too bad, because they are really missing a lot of the satisfactions of living in the country. You can't learn much about country ways if you stick to yourself and import all your friends from the city. Also, you won't pick up special little tricks, such as putting skunk cabbage leaves around tomato plants to keep cut worms away, until you reach the point where you can have a casual chat with a neighbor about tomatoes, cut worms, and gardening in general. You won't learn the very best time of year to buy native apples, or the name of the farmer who has good topsoil to sell cheap, or why everyone in town turns out for the Democratic party barbeque, but the Republicans always get elected, until you get to know the community and the names of all the players.

Country people are very much like other people in that they are individuals and not all the same. Some will have backgrounds and interests far different from yours, while you will have much more in common with others. Some have supper at 5:30, and most have finished by 7:00. Some live in expensive houses, and some live in very primitive dwellings and sometimes in trailers or mobile houses. Some want the community to go in one direction, others insist it should go in another. Some will be all for "progress and growth," regardless of what it costs the community in aesthetic values, and some will want to stop the clock or even turn it back to life of a generation or two ago.

A country community is very like a large family. It may not always be a happy family, and the individuals in it may often be at odds with one another, will criticize one another in public as well as in private, make fun of one another at times, and even call one another some pretty harsh names. But to outsiders, they usually present a united front, especially if the outsider is critical of any of the relatives. Until you become a member of the family yourself, it's a good idea to keep your criticisms to a minimum, if indeed you voice any at all.

There may be things you don't approve of or like in the community, and there may be a lot of things you don't understand. One thing that city people often can't understand is that most country people feel strongly about their right to have a gun and are very much against gun control laws—despite the awful tragedies that have happened in America because of guns. It's quite pointless to get into a discussion with them about this because:

(1) They don't live in crowded cities.
(2) They don't usually shoot other people or each other with their guns, except accidentally.
(3) They are more often law-abiding than not.
(4) They believe that a man's home is his castle and that a man has a right to protect his property.
(5) They like to hunt.

The opening of the hunting season is a big event in the country, and a great many men and boys hunt as a matter of course. Some because they enjoy it as a sport and like to vary their diets from time to time with a little venison, wild pig, or wild birds. Others hunt because they need the game as food. If you don't approve of hunting, that is your privilege, but you'll be wise not to start preaching to the country folk about the evils of hunting or owning a gun. And just because you may see a lot of bumper stickers with such slogans as "Get Rid of the Reds—Not the Guns" each time some gun control legislation comes up, it doesn't mean the town is loaded with vigilantes. It's their way of saying that in this instance, anyway, they want to maintain the status quo.

The status quo to them includes being able to hunt in the same places they have hunted all their lives. This might happen to be—as of the time you took title to it—your property. And you may not want people hunting on your property. But if that property has always been open to local hunters, and you immediately plaster it with No Hunting and No Trespassing signs, you are going to be classified as the type of city person the countryside can do without. If you want to keep the goodwill of the community, the best thing to do is to forget the signs. Many farmers, of course, actually encourage local hunters to hunt their property, not to totally eliminate the wildlife, but to keep the population down and the animals from destroying their crops. Or they may do it just to be accommodating.

Most country people are not as concerned with keeping others off their property as are city or suburban people. In the suburbs, for instance, you probably would not walk across someone's property without asking permission, but in the country you probably would just go ahead and do it if that was the shortest way to get where you were going. Keep Off signs, especially, are not appreciated and are sometimes interpreted as a slap in the face by the Old Timers. One family we know was never considered anything but "city people," even though they had lived in the community for fifteen years, because when they first arrived they had fenced off and posted a small pond where local children had been allowed to swim and fish for as long as anybody could remember.

While local inhabitants are usually quite willing to share the attractions of their property with their fellow townspeople, they still have a strong sense of ownership of their land. They and their families may have lived on the land for generations, and the one thing that really gets their hackles up is for city people to criticize or look down their noses at the use to which they put their property—whether it is allowing the piling up of rusted-out trucks and automobiles in their front yards, or choosing to live in a trailer or mobile home in full view of the road. While the junk cars certainly are eyesores, they may be there because the owner hopes to sell or use the parts, and he may be living in the mobile home because it is the only kind of housing that he can afford. A tumble-down house without inside plumbing may be more picturesque, but it's not as comfortable a place to raise a family. There's not much you can do about these problems until you become part of the community and become involved in community affairs, and maybe not even then. In the meantime, try to keep your negative reactions to yourself.

Another good way to make an enemy of an Old Timer is to give him the benefit of your superior knowledge of conservation and ecology. Indeed, you may be more aware of these problems than your country fellows and can certainly, on your own land, put this knowledge to good use. Hopefully, you can, in time, be active in awakening the community to whatever ecological or conservation problems may be detrimental to the public good, but in the beginning, you'll be a lot better off if you just observe. Sometimes, too, you can expose your ignorance rather than your erudition by jumping in before you know what it is all about. We are reminded of some new property owners from the city who became irate at what they thought was indiscriminate destruction of trees in a neighboring farmer's back wood lot. They wrote an impassioned letter to the local newspaper which, much to their later dismay, was printed. It turned out that the farmer was just thinning out the wood lot so that the remaining trees would have room and sufficient sunlight to grow. The whole town had a good laugh at their expense.

City people can often be amazingly insensitive to things that affect the very livelihood of others. A young couple we know—nice kids, fresh from the city—were telling a farmer, who was dead tired from hauling water to keep his crops from dying during a long drought, that they were praying it wouldn't rain for the next few days because they were planning to go sailing. It wasn't that they were callous; they just hadn't thought.

Country people are sometimes considered "clannish," and they are, in a sense. They've known each other all their lives, and their families have probably known each other or intermarried for generations. Related or not, they have many common interests, and it's only natural that they gravitate toward each other. They also stick together because in the country you are far more your brother's keeper than in the city, and things that happen can touch the lives of everyone. In the city, for instance, if you hear a fire siren, unless it happens on your block, it just means that there's a fire someplace. A fire siren in the country means more than just a fire—it means that a neighbor's or a relative's house or barn is burning—and it becomes a very personal matter to everyone in the community. In the city, fires have street addresses. In the country, they have proper names: the Jones house, the Smith barn, or the Dombroski general store.

People keep an eye on each other's property—not so much out of curiosity as concern. In our area, where winters can be very bitter, many households have a little gadget that you put in a window, facing the road or a neighbor's place, in case you have to leave the house for a day or more. If your heating system fails, the gadget blinks a warning light that alerts whoever is checking your house that the heat is off and to please do something about it before the place gets so cold that the pipes freeze.

One of the nice things, to us, about small towns and country living today, is the diversity of people who may live within a few miles of each other. Unlike the suburbs, where most people who live in the same neighborhood have more or less similar backgrounds and incomes and are often even in the same age group, there is a tremendous variation within a small community. You might have a retired banker and your telephone lineman on one side of the road; a middle-aged college professor and a beginning house painter on the other; with a no-special-age shopkeeper and an aging artist up the road; and so on. Nice as this is, though, people sometimes do odd things at odd times of the day or night which can be disturbing. Where we live, some of our fellow residents sometimes take it into their heads to cut wood with a chain saw on Sunday afternoons, an earsplitting sound if there ever was one. If this happened in the suburbs, you might get a group of neighbors together and make a joint plea to the chain saw jockey to stop disturbing the neighborhood. You could conceivably even call the police and ask them to have it stopped, but not in the country. If a man wants to chain saw on Sunday afternoon, it's his God-given right, and the best thing you can do is to just let it go at that. Who knows, you might want to do some chain-sawing on a Sunday afternoon yourself someday.

chapter 11
THE COUNTRY CAR

They say that old Henry Ford changed the way of life for the rural American when he started to mass produce the Model "T." One thing he did for certain was to make country people absolutely dependent on the automobile. City people don't need a car for day-to-day living, and even suburban people can get along without one if they can afford taxis and can put up with buses and trains. But in the country a car is a must. There aren't any buses, except the school bus, and the nearest taxi might be ten miles away in another township. You not only need a car, but you need one that runs all the time, because when it isn't running, you are stuck.

What's the best kind of car to have in the country? We'd say the simpler the better. The fewer gadgets on the car, the fewer things there are to get out of order, and the easier it is to fix, if something goes wrong. Light pickup trucks and jeeps are popular with country people because they are simple. They don't have a lot of unnecessary gadgets, they've got enough power to get in and out of tough places, and they have a lot of road clearance. Plenty of distance between the car and the road is good, because while you may live on a paved road, you may have occasion to go on a road that isn't paved. Just a couple of ruts with the average family car or station wagon, and you'll scrape the undercarriage, maybe pull something like the exhaust pipe or muffler off, or just plain get hung up. A small pickup truck is also handy for hauling stuff—anything from a load of wood or brush to a small piano.

We believe that when it comes to buying a car for the country you'll want to be more concerned with the availability of good service than with the brand of car. If the only service station in the area specializes in Fords, we'd buy a Ford. If the guy handles Chevys, we'd buy a Chevy. Any car is going to need servicing from time to time, and it will also need new parts, so the closer the service, the better. There's also the goodwill aspect. Maybe you already had a car when you moved into the community, and a new one is not in your immediate future. Okay, but at least buy your gas and oil from your local dealer, so that if one morning Old Faithful just won't start, he will know who you are when you call for help.

Stay clear of sports cars and complicated foreign cars, unless you have someone nearby who can service them, or can do it yourself. A neighbor of ours has a very fine and expensive foreign car, and when it runs it's great. But when it doesn't run he's got a problem, because the local garage not only doesn't know how to fix it but doesn't have the parts to fix it with.

The exception to the foreign car rule is, of course, the VW Bug. There are enough of these around so that just about every garage mechanic has had experience tinkering with them, and they are also so simple that even if he's never seen one before, it doesn't take him long to figure out what makes it tick and why it isn't ticking.

Anyone who lives any distance at all from a garage should learn to do a few repairs when necessary. Nothing complicated, mind you, but things like being able to clean the points if they get so dirty that the car won't start or how to dry them off if they become wet after a long, heavy rain.

You also need a little special equipment for your car, plus a bit of old-fashioned know-how. You should learn, for instance, how to change a tire. If you want to refresh your knowledge, buy a good jack. Don't depend on those pieces of junk they often include with cars these days. If you don't feel up to changing a tire, get one of those compressed-air tire inflaters and keep it handy. This will at least inflate the tire so you can drive to a garage to get it fixed, rather than having to pay for a service truck to come to your place.

Buy the best grade of battery that you can afford, for in cold weather you'll need all the juice you can get, unless you keep your car in a heated garage or live in a mild climate. And you'd better keep a set of jump wires on hand so that if your battery does go dead, you can start the car, provided there is another car handy, a neighbor's perhaps. In cold areas, unless you do a lot of driving every day, you may find it worthwhile to buy a battery charger. These run on household current and cost around fifteen dollars. We never had to buy one because our neighbor has one, and it's saved the day on many occasions.

Where winters are very severe, people often use those electric immersion heaters that are inserted into the engine through the oil dripstick tube. They keep the oil warm enough so that when you step on the starter the engine can turn over with relative ease. If you don't want to bother with one of these, a heat lamp can be used to warm up an icy engine.

You'll be wise to keep a couple of road flares in your glove compartment or someplace in the car, because a breakdown on an unlighted, country road can be dangerous. In addition, keep a flashlight in the car.

We also suggest that you keep a reserve can of gasoline at your place—not in the house, of course. Country service stations often close up early in the evening and aren't always open on Sunday. Keep five gallons of gas outside in one of those surplus GI gasoline and water containers.

Driving on back country roads isn't quite the same as driving on a turnpike or thruway. The roads are often quite narrow and winding, and you can't always see what is coming from other directions until you're about to pass. If you meet a large truck and are going too fast, you'll either sideswipe, or you'll go onto the shoulder and may get stuck or worse. So take it easy on speed. And you've also got to expect to have to stop suddenly when you come around a curve and find a school bus, a kid playing, a dog, a deer, or a nice, slow-moving tractor.

In winter, they don't always get back country roads as free of ice and snow as the main roads, so you'd better be prepared for this kind of driving if you live in a cold area. You should, of course, have snow tires, but even these don't do too much good on ice. Winter driving requires a lot of caution, and you have to be constantly alert for the unexpected, such as a patch of ice under a bridge or underpass.

chapter 12
SECURITY

One reason why many city people are heading for the woods these days is they are just plain scared of the city. Well, there's no doubt that there is far less violence in the country than in the city, and the country can be a peaceful place. Sad but true, however, the days when you could leave your front door unlocked, allow any stranger to come in to use the phone, or invite him in for a drink of water are rapidly fading away. The country is a far safer place than the average city or even the suburbs, but it's not completely safe—and maybe it never was.

Of course, a lot of things that will give you or your city children the creeps are just plain country sounds. Country quiet can be pretty noisy at times, and a country house can be a noisy house, especially in the still of night. It is then you'll be able to hear a lot of sounds that you ordinarily wouldn't notice in the daytime because of background noises that mask them. And they will often be considerably magnified by your imagination. That thumping downstairs in the middle of the night may be nothing more than your dog scratching a flea or a crew of field mice trying to find where you hid the Ivory soap (they love Ivory soap). And what may sound to you like an elephant stomping around on the roof may only be a squirrel up past his bedtime, or a tree branch scraping against the siding or a rain gutter. The house itself will make a lot of noise. It will groan and creak at times, especially if there is a high wind. If it has an ancient plumbing or heating system, you can expect strange rumblings and bangings from time to time. You had better get used to these sounds as soon as you can if you want to stay happy and get a good night's sleep.

It's especially important for the children not to be concerned about these noises. Even if the sounds may worry you at first, don't let on to the kids that they are anything more than just some little animal out looking for his supper, or the wind playing with the branch of a tree. The first time you hear a hoot owl in the middle of the night it may scare the daylights out of you, but don't show it. Try to make it a special event so that the children will actually look forward to hearing that old owl hoot again some other night.

Owning A Dog: If you are going to have a dog or dogs, the country is the place to do it, but there are a few potential problems to be mindful of. A country dog, unless fenced in, is almost bound to roam at times and may end up in trouble. If a female and in heat, she'll roam and end up a mother. If you keep her chained or fenced in during this delicate time, you'll have a lot of strange male dogs about. It's usually simpler to put her in a kennel for as long as she is in heat—around three weeks—but that is, of course, an additional expense you may not want to take on at the time. Most "dog" people advise either breeding a female—if she is purebred and you're up to handling the responsibilities of the whelping and the puppies—or having the dog spayed. You can usually sell purebred pups for a good price, but if you have qualms about either course, you're better off with a male.

A major hazard with country dogs is that they are not as aware of car traffic as city dogs, who are usually on a leash anyway. They will get on the road, and a high percentage of country dogs are killed or seriously hurt by cars. Some dogs just naturally roam more than others, and these are the ones who most often get killed. Beagles, for example, like to run all over the countryside and often get hit. If you decide on a dog, avoid the hunting breeds that like to roam, unless you want to worry all the time or can train the dog to stay home.

Dogs are a responsibility, because you just can't take off for a weekend, or even for a long day, unless you have someone to look after the pup. In the city, you can find dog-sitters and dog-walkers, but this is not always true in the country. However, there are advantages, too, and they often outweigh the disadvantages. A dog can offer a certain degree of protection from intruders, especially if it is a large animal. It doesn't matter if the dog wouldn't hurt a fly. If it is big enough to look as if it could deliver a nasty bite, it will be somewhat effective. If the dog barks at strangers (our dog barks mostly at people she knows and likes), that's good too. It's nice to have a little warning when someone approaches your house, especially when you are alone. But most important, a dog is good company and a good companion for children, and it's hard to think of living in the country without having a dog—and even a cat.

How About A Gun: Having a gun in the house really comes down to whether or not you are prepared to use it. If a rabid fox, raccoon, or dog comes around your house, you aren't going to get rid of it by firing a warning shot across its bow. You've got to shoot it and kill it. The same thing holds true in relation to human intruders. In a showdown, you've got to be prepared to shoot, and if not to kill, at least to put the intruder out of commission. And you've got to make this so apparent that the intruder knows it and gets out before you have to shoot. If you don't make it quite obvious that you mean serious business, he can as easily as not just walk over and take the gun right out of your hands. You've got to act as if you not only know how to use a gun, but that you have used it and are about to use it right then and there.

Most police officers suggest you don't keep a gun in the house, saying that it will do more harm than good. We aren't sure. We keep a rifle in a handy closet, and it does give a certain sense of security. The last time we fired it was a couple of years ago, when we tried to scare a big, fat woodchuck from our vegetable garden. It didn't do much good, so we finally had to put up a fence.

If you are going to have a gun and aren't an authority in these matters, get a rifle, or better yet, a shotgun. Don't get a handgun (a pistol) because—aside from the fact that it's hard to even hit the side of a barn with one—they are dangerous to have around a house, especially if there are children, and you forget to keep it under lock and key.

Preventing Burglary: One reason it doesn't really pay to keep a gun is that the typical burglar isn't going to come around if he knows someone is at home. When you read about someone who has a confrontation with a burglar in his house or apartment, it's either because the intruder figured no one was at home and made a serious mistake, or because there was something of such great value—a suitcase full of money or a drawer full of rare jewels—that is was worth taking the risk. But country burglars are not international jewel thieves. Many of them are junkies (yes, even in the country) out to get something they can sell for enough money for a fix, or local kids who reason that they have a better use for your portable TV than you have, or are burglarizing just for kicks.

Not too many years ago, burglary was so rare in the country that most people never bothered to lock their doors, even when they went away for several days. In those days of yore, you could leave almost anything lying around the grounds, and no one would bother it—or at least most of the time they wouldn't. But things are somewhat different today, and while the country is far safer than the city, burglaries do occur, and with increasing frequency.

As we said, most burglars won't go near a house if they believe someone is at home, so the trick is to always make the house appear occupied, even when it isn't. You can make a family game out of this. For example, when you leave the house during the day, always close the garage door so that it will appear that the car is still inside. If you didn't pull up the window shades or draperies when you got up, do it before you leave, because if shades are down during the day, it tells someone that you are probably not at home. You might even leave the radio on, just to add to the illusion.

When you go out in the evening, don't do what so many people do, which is to turn out all the lights, and leave the light on over the front door. Leave a few lights burning inside the house—in the kitchen, living room, and other areas that would normally be occupied. But be sure to pull the shades down, so that no one can see in from the outside.

Those electric timers are handy things to have to make an empty house appear occupied. They can be set to turn lights on and off at given times. With a couple of these, you can leave the house for weeks at a time, and it will appear occupied at night. When it gets dark, the kitchen and living room lights go on. Later, the bedroom lights go on and those in the kitchen and living room go off. Pretty soon only a hall or bathroom light is on, and the next day the entire script is repeated.

You should have good locks on your doors and windows. Use a deadbolt-type lock on doors and keyed locks on windows.

About the best way we've found to prevent burglaries is to keep our neighbors informed of our movements, so that when we are away for the day, or longer, they'll keep an eye on the house. And we do the same for them. Burglars don't work just at night. A lot of them work during the day and drive around in delivery trucks. They'll drive up to a house that looks as if no one is home and ring the doorbell. If someone answers, they'll say they are looking for such and such an address and go on their way. If no one answers their knock, they'll try the door, and if it doesn't open, they'll open the lock with a strip of plastic, unless it's a deadbolt lock. After that it's easy. Go inside, see what's worth taking, and load it into the truck. And unless your neighbor happens to know that you aren't at home and are not expecting any deliveries, he or she may watch the entire operation and not know that you're being robbed. So look out for your neighbor and see that he looks out for you.

Children's Fun and Games: If you knew what your children were doing when they are out playing, you'd probably be frightened out of your wits, because the country offers some wonderful and exciting opportunities for kids to live more or less dangerously. We are both, in a way, country children and know the delights of hanging from a railroad trestle as the train passes overhead or discovering a box of dynamite in an old, abandoned quarry. But we made it, and so did most of our little friends, with only a minor accident here and there.

A normal, healthy child is bound to explore, so maybe you should explore together—first to see what he or she could get into, and then maybe lay down the law. If you don't know that there is an abandoned mine, a flooded quarry, a deserted factory, or some other potential hazard, you can't tell the kids not to go there, and if you don't tell them they can't, they probably will. If they are reasonably normal or adventurous, they may go anyway, but at least you'll have some idea where to look for them.

chapter **13**

KNOWING YOUR HOUSE
AND HOW TO HANDLE IT

One of the first items on the agenda after you have bought a house is to find out as much about it as you can. The more you know about the house—what makes it tick or not tick—the better. Such knowledge will not only make it easier to take care of the house, but make it possible for you to do a lot of repairs and maintenance yourself, and also avoid a lot of headaches and expense.

No two houses are exactly the same. Even if they look alike, they won't act alike, so while you'll be able to get a lot of general information on the care and repair of houses by reading some of the excellent books on these subjects, you'll have to go right to the horse's mouth to get specific information on your house, assuming that you can find a well-informed horse.

A good horse to begin with is the previous owner. He can tell you a lot about the house, and he is more apt to tell you about its eccentricities now that you own the place than he was when you were a prospective buyer. Never forget that the seller or his broker is not legally bound to point out flaws in a house to a prospective buyer. If they are asked a direct question, and they know the answer, they are supposed to tell the truth, but if they aren't asked, or if they are allowed to change the subject, they can't be held responsible. You'll generally find that after he has his money, the seller can be very loquacious and may tell you more about the house than you care to know.

Start off by asking for the names of local mechanics who are familiar with the house and its equipment. This would include the plumber, electrician, heating service outfit, the people who have cleaned or installed the septic tank, and so forth. You are usually better off to stick with people who are already familiar with a particular element of the house than to have to pay a new person who has to learn how things are put together before he can even begin to fix it. (That is, unless you have reason to believe that the particular mechanic or serviceman made a great botch of things in the first place.) Also, if the seller or his broker is unable to give you sufficient information about the various components of the house, the men who have done work on it can.

Here are a few of the more important things that you should be familiar with from the very start.

Water Supply: In the country, people get their water from wells, cisterns, springs, and ponds. As a general rule, you won't have the abundant supply of water that you had in the city or the suburbs. If you use it too freely, you may run out; so find out all you can about the capacity of the system. You should also have the water supply analyzed for purity and mineral content. If the water has a high bacteria count, you should either use bottled water or boil your drinking water until you can correct the situation. If the water contains large amounts of iron, sulpher, etc., you may need to put in water-conditioning equipment to make it suitable for use. Your County Agent can tell you where to go to have your water tested.

Wells: These are the most common source for water in the country. There are two kinds of wells: a shallow well and a deep well. A shallow well is no more than twenty-five feet deep, and the water supply can be easily contaminated by either surface water or by a nearby septic system or cesspool. Shallow wells may often go dry at certain times of the year when there is little rainfall. On the other hand, some of them are excellent. We share a shallow well with our neighbor. It's a dug-well, only about sixteen-feet deep but has never gone dry or even shown a marked decrease in water level. But the people who own the house next door to our neighbor's have a lot of trouble with their well going dry.

The best advice we can give you about a shallow well is to live with it a year or so, keeping an eye on the water level, before you start adding water-consuming things like another bathroom, a sink garbage disposal unit, or underground lawn sprinkling system.

A deep well—it may be several hundred feet deep—is much less likely to become contaminated than a shallow well and seldom goes dry. But they can. If you want to find out about the deep well on your property, get the name of the outfit that drilled it. Most well drillers today keep a log of each job, and this tells the depth of the well and the number of gallons a minute it produces. A minimum of five gallons is okay, but anything less than this probably means that you'll have to ration your water to some degree.

With either type of well, shallow or deep, you will have a pump and a storage tank. Find out the brand of pump and who services it, because sooner or later it will require some attention.

Cisterns are large tanks, usually underground, that are filled with water from springs or even from rainwater falling from the roof. How much water they will supply depends on their capacity, and the amount of water that the spring provides, or the amount of rainfall. It's a makeshift arrangement at best, designed for a time when people didn't use much water, and if you have one of them, you'd better start saving your pennies toward a deep well.

Lakes seldom go dry, but ponds can, and the water from both can be easily contaminated and can taste pretty unpleasant at times.

Sewage System: Unless you have a town sewage system, this is going to be either a cesspool or septic tank. Both of these are set underground, except in certain special circumstances where a septic tank will be set above ground, because ledge rock prevents it from being set below. You want to find out which you have—cesspool or septic system—and the location. When you find out where it is placed, mark the spot with a good-sized stake, so that you or someone else can find it if there is trouble.

A cesspool is just a big hole in the ground, lined with stone or masonry block, with a lid on the top. All waste from the house flows into it, and the liquid matter is absorbed into the surrounding soil. It's a very primitive and unsanitary arrangement. Cesspools can be a big nuisance, because during heavy rains they can overflow and allow sewage to back up into the house drainage system. The result will be an overflowing toilet, or worse. Cesspools may also overflow when they become too full of solid waste, when the soil around them can no longer absorb moisture, or when the soil becomes saturated with grease from the kitchen sink drain. When a cesspool overflows, about all you can do is have it pumped out. It may work for a time, or it may overflow again almost immediately. The best policy is to have it replaced with a septic tank. The next best thing is to dig a new cesspool near the old one and connect the two together.

A septic system is far superior to a cesspool. It is more sanitary and, if properly maintained, will operate effectively for years and years. You should have the system inspected at least once a year by a professional cleaning outfit and have the tank cleaned when necessary. Cleaning is usually required every two or three years, but if the system is too small, the job may have to be done every year to keep the system in proper condition.

By the way, the runoff from the house roof should never be connected to the cesspool or septic system, because a heavy rain will cause them to overflow. The best way to handle the rainwater coming from roof downspouts or leaders is to run it into a dry well—same thing as a cesspool but used just for rainwater.

The Plumbing System: Get the former owner, or a plumber, to check you out on this, unless you can figure it out for yourself. You want to know if you have copper or galvanized iron pipe in the house. If you can see the pipes, you will know which is which, because the galvanized pipe is a silver color. Copper is preferable, because the galvanized stuff will rust eventually, or fill up with mineral deposits so that the flow through the lines becomes only a trickle. Galvanized iron pipes will also produce rusty water, especially out of the hot-water taps.

You want to find out the location of the main shut-off valve, so you can cut off all the water inside the house in case of a bad leak. You should also locate the shut-off valves to the various branches of the system. It's a smart idea to tag these valves so that if you are not around and there is trouble, whoever is there will know which valve to turn.

If you live in an area where below-freezing temperatures occur, find out if there are pipes running outside the house to any outbuilding, garden water spigots, etc. These should be turned off and drained in winter to prevent them from freezing and bursting.

Hot water is supplied either by separate hot-water heaters running on electricity, bottled gas, or oil, or by a coil in the boiler used for heating the house in winter. It won't take long to find out the capacity of your hot-water system. About the first time you run a bath or take a long shower you'll know if you have an adequate supply of hot water. If you have a heater that is independent of your boiler and you don't have enough hot water, you can replace the existing heater with a larger unit or have an additional unit installed. You can get some pretty good deals on hot-water heaters these days, because a lot of fuel and electric outfits rent them for a nominal fee if you use their fuel—whether electricity, gas, or oil. They'll even install the unit and service it for nothing.

If the hot water comes from a boiler coil, and you don't have enough, you can either have a storage tank installed or have an independent hot-water heater installed. Electric, gas, and oil heaters are all fine. The only thing that should affect your choice is which is going to cost you the least to have installed and to operate.

You might keep in mind that it takes less water, both hot and cold, to take a shower than it does to take a bath. If you have a limited amount of water, you should encourage all members of the family to take short showers, instead of soaking in a full tub.

Minor Repairs: You should learn how to do a lot of small, plumbing repair jobs, such as fixing a leaky faucet by replacing the washer or the packing, clearing a stopped-up drain or toilet bowl, adjusting or replacing the flush mechanism inside the toilet flush tank, and so forth. Any good book on home repairs will tell you how to handle these jobs.

Heating System: If your house has a heating system, it may be one of several types. The most common are electric, forced warm air, circulating hot water, and steam.

Electric: We'll start off with electric heat, because it doesn't require much in the way of description, and even less in the way of maintenance. Heat is supplied by electric coils in baseboard units, or set into wall and ceiling panels. There isn't much that can go wrong with the system, and about the only maintenance required is to vacuum baseboard units from time to time to remove dust and dirt.

Electric heat can cost you an arm and a leg to operate, however, unless the house has been thoroughly insulated and heat loss is reduced to a minimum. This means tight-

fitting storm windows or insulating glass, weather stripping, and no open joints or seams that will allow warm air
in the house to escape. If you find your heating costs are
excessive, get hold of your utility company and have them
send someone around to check out the house and see what
needs to be done to cut down on the operating costs.
Compared to other types of energy—oil and natural gas—
electricity is expensive, and you don't want to waste it if
you can possibly help it. If you have other difficulties with
your electric heating system, contact your utility company
or an electrical contractor.

All other types of systems—forced warm air, circulating
hot water, and steam—are fueled by either gas or oil. If
you don't know anyone who can explain exactly how your
system works, ask the outfit that delivers your fuel oil or
your gas company to send someone over to explain the
operation to you. Most plumbers, by the way, are familiar
with hot water and steam systems.

Forced Warm Air: Here you have a furnace that heats the
air which is then pushed through ducts to the various
areas of the house by means of a blower. There are filters
inside the furnace to remove dirt from the air, and these
filters must be cleaned or replaced when they become
dirty. The usual method of determining when a filter is
dirty is to hold it up to the light. If you can't see light
through it, clean it or replace it. Have someone show you
how this is done, along with how and when to oil the
blower and blower motor and how to replace the blower
fan belt.

Some forced warm air systems make a terrific amount
of noise. Most of this is due to improper installation.

Circulating Hot Water: With this system you have a boiler
in which water is heated then pumped through pipes to
radiators, convectors, baseboard units, or even coils set
into the floor. There is a good deal to learn about how to

operate this kind of system. As far as the boiler goes, you want to know whether it has an automatic feed, so that water is added automatically when required, or if it is a hand operation, which means someone has to open a valve on the water feed line to add water to the boiler. You need to know how to tell when the boiler is full, and if there is something called a low-water cutoff that will turn off the burner, if for any reason there isn't sufficient water in the boiler.

With this system, all the pipes, radiators, etc., along with the boiler, must be full of water, if the system is to operate properly. Now and then, pockets of air will get trapped in some of the radiators, etc., and this will keep them from heating properly. On each radiator, baseboard unit, etc., there is a little air valve that can be opened to allow the air to escape. You should have someone explain how this is done, because it will probably need doing several times during the course of the year.

Steam: These systems are pretty old-fashioned but will work well if in good repair and properly cared for. They have a boiler, and you want to find out how to tell when there is the correct amount of water in it and how to add water if necessary. Check to see if it has an automatic feed and low-water cutoff. On most steam boilers there is a little glass water gauge which will usually be marked to indicate the correct water level, but not always. If it has a gauge, find out the correct level and mark it yourself with a little paint or nail polish. Steam boilers require the addition of water much more frequently than hot-water boilers.

With a steam system the radiators will be either cold or very hot, depending on whether the steam is coming up or not. And the steam comes up only when the burner is on. At one end of each radiator you'll find a little air valve, and this is supposed to open when the steam starts coming up so that the air inside the radiator can escape. If the air doesn't escape, there is no room for the steam, so the radiator remains cold. These little air valves have to be replaced from time to time for they get old and don't work, and that means the radiator will be cold. Some valves are adjustable so you can set them to allow certain radiators to heat up faster than others.

The water in steam boilers can get very dirty, and this can reduce the efficiency of the heating system. You should find out how to flush out the boiler when required.

Gas Burners: If the furnace or boiler is gas-fired you don't have much to worry about, because gas burners are very simple and seldom require much maintenance. Sometimes the pilot light goes out, and you should learn how to light it. There are usually instructions on how to do this right on the furnace or boiler. You should also learn how to work the main valve manually, if there is a manual valve, so that the burner will operate, even if there is no electric power. Your chance of having a gas burner in the country, however, is rather remote. They don't run gas mains out in the boondocks, and bottled gas is far too expensive to heat a home. If you don't have electric heat, chances are you'll heat with oil.

Oil Burners: These are much more complicated than a gas burner and need to be checked out at least once a year—in the summer or early fall, before a new heating season begins. The older burners can be a serious problem, for they can get to a point where they break down at the drop of a hat. You'd be wise to get a new burner, rather than fool around with the old one. The best place to buy one is from the outfit that delivers your fuel oil. They have good units, will usually give you a pretty good price, and will see that the burner works. Remember that it's to their advantage for your burner to operate. They are in the business of selling fuel oil, and a burner that doesn't run, doesn't burn any oil.

Oil burners are tricky, and you don't want to try and

fool with one yourself, or let anyone other than an expert tinker with it. You should know, however, the location of the emergency switch, so that if the house catches on fire or the burner goes wild and just keeps running after it should have turned itself off, you can cut off the power to it. You should also learn how to reset the stack switch which is inside a little metal box attached to the stovepipe that runs from the furnace or boiler to the chimney. This little switch is designed to turn off the burner if, for one reason or another, the fuel oil being pumped into the combustion chamber does not ignite within a certain interval. Often, however, this delicate switch will turn off or keep the burner off for no good reason. You can generally start things up again if you know how to flick the little switch button. And if this doesn't do any good, give the little metal box that contains the switch a light tap with your hand.

Thermostat: This is the little gadget set on the wall that tells the heating system when to send up heat. If the thermostat is old or doesn't work properly, you'll have no end of trouble getting the proper amount of heat in the house. You also want to make sure that the thermostat is not set on a wall where it can be exposed to cold drafts—this will make it demand heat when it isn't required—or near a lamp or other heat, for this will keep it from demanding heat when it really is required. We once knew a family who moved into a large country house and couldn't understand why in winter the house was always cold when they had a dinner party. Turned out that the thermostat was on one of the walls in the dining room directly above a sideboard. When the family had a dinner party they lit the candles on the sideboard, and these gave off enough heat to keep the thermostat from working properly.

Space Heaters: In some houses, especially those in warmer climates, you won't find central heat but instead, one or two space heaters around the house. If these are electric you don't have any problem, but the ones that burn a fuel—gas or oil—can be a hazard, for the heater not only consumes oxygen from the air but, unless the heater is vented, can give off dangerous fumes. Many communities do not allow heaters of this type because they are so dangerous, especially if there are children or elderly people in the house. If you have them, replace them with electric heaters or with a central system.

Electric Wiring: You should find out if you have 120 volts or 240 volts, because if you have only 120 volts, you can't use appliances or equipment requiring 240 volts, such as kitchen ranges, certain air conditioners, and clothes dryers. You can get this information from the previous owner, an electrician, or from the guy from the utility company who comes to read the meter.

You also want to know the location and how to operate the main electric switch which may be used, if necessary, to cut off all power to the house. If there is a circuit breaker panel, you should find out how to reset a circuit if the switch has blown because of a short or overload. If the house has a fuse box, find out how to change a fuse. You should also have spare fuses on hand for all the branch circuits, as well as a couple of the large main fuses.

If you haven't yet learned how to replace a lamp cord, fix appliance plugs, and all the rest of these little electric chores, it would be a good idea to learn now. You can get most of the information you need in any good home repair book.

The Basement: If the house has a basement, it may get pretty wet in a rainy period or a sudden thaw. If this is the case, there may already be a "sump pump." But if there is not, you might need one. A sump pump is an electrically-driven pump that is set in a pit in the floor of the basement. The idea is that if the pit fills with water, the pump automatically goes on and pumps the water out as fast as it flows in. If you find such a pump, check it out to see that it really will run. You can do this by raising the rod that connects a float in the pit to the pump. If the pump doesn't work, better have it fixed or get a new one. If there is no sump pump, and you find indications that the basement does get wet—water stains on the walls and floor, rust on the base of the furnace, the boiler, or other metal equipment that rests on the floor—better install a sump pump. This is a much safer and less costly solution to your problem than trying to waterproof the basement walls and floors. You might also want to check around to see if you can find the source of the trouble. Often it's due to improper grading around the house, which allows water to collect near the basement walls, or to the fact that the downspouts or leaders from the gutters dump the water right at the foundation walls instead of being connected to underground pipes that carry the water a safe distance from the basement.

Crawl Space: Some houses don't have basements, just crawl space between the ground and the floor. There should be openings in the foundation wall so that air can circulate in this space, for if not, the house may become damp. The openings should be covered with heavy screening to keep out rodents.

Floors: You should know what material the floor covering is made of, so you can take proper care of it. The floors in many older houses, for example, are covered with asphalt tile, and if you use a floor wax that contains a solvent on these, you will ruin them. The only safe floor wax to use on asphalt tile is the water-base self-polishing type.

Roofs: If you can find out how old the roof covering is, this will give you a clue as to when you might expect trouble with leaks or have to reroof. Most roofs are covered with wood or asphalt shingles. Wood shingles will last about twenty-odd years and asphalt about fifteen years. The roof covering on the south side of the house ages about one-third faster than the north side. Lots of country people play it smart and just reroof the side that needs it and let the other side alone until it has to be replaced.

Some country houses have tin roofs, and when these begin to leak from rust spots, they can usually be fixed by coating with a roofing compound composed of aluminum flakes and asphalt. The stuff is easy to apply, doesn't cost much, and does a good job unless the metal is very badly rusted.

Gutters and Downspouts: You have to keep gutters free of tree leaves and other debris or you'll run into trouble. Clean them out once a year, in the fall after the leaves are off the trees. You can save yourself having to do this job if you install gutter guards, wire-mesh screening, over the tops of the gutters.

In cold areas, snow and ice often collect in the gutters and along the eaves and may allow water to back up under the shingles and get into the house. The way to fix this is to install electric heating cables in the gutters or along the eaves. You can get these cables at most hardware and electric stores.

Exterior Paint: Ask the previous owner when the house was last painted and with what kind of paint, oil or latex, and stick with that type when you repaint. The average outside paint job will last around five years. If you wait too long before repainting, the old paint film will become so thin that you may need two coats, rather than one coat, to do the job. It will cost around $750.00 to have the average two-bedroom house painted by professionals. The larger the house, the more expensive. Most country people either do the job themselves or wait until summer when they can hire high school or college kids who will do the work for a lot less. And there is no rule that says the entire house has to be painted at one time or even in the same year. It's not unusual to find someone who paints one side of his house one year and then doesn't get around to doing another section until the following year, when he has the time or the money to do it.

Insulation: You want to find out if the house has been insulated and if so, the thickness of the insulation. Insulation will help keep the house cooler in summer and warmer in winter. You should have about six inches of insulation at the top of the house, either on the underside of the roof or in the attic floor. If the walls of the house are not insulated, it might be worth having an insulating company come over and give you a bid on what it will cost to blow the stuff into the wall cavity.

Screens and Storm Windows: In just about every area you will need window screens in summer to keep out insects. In cold areas you will need storm windows to cut heat loss and save fuel. A good many houses today have combination screen-and-windows that are permanently installed. But many older homes still have the old-fashioned wood screens and storm windows, and each spring you have to take down the storm windows and put up the screens. What makes this job time-consuming and irritating, aside from the fact that you might have to work while standing on a ladder, is that each screen or storm window may be a little different and will only fit one particular window frame. Unless you know which one goes where, you, or someone you hire, can spend hours using the trial and error method. See if you can get the previous owner to show you any identifying marks on the frames so you will know which one goes where. If there aren't any such marks, make them yourself when you are taking down the screens or storm windows. It's easy while you're about it, and you'll be glad you did. And if there are no screens or storm windows, you'd better get some. This is a good thing to check when you first take possession of your house, because if you buy them at that time, the cost is added to the purchase price, which is handy for tax purposes.

Termites: Just about everyone has heard about these little insects, and the very mention of them is enough to make most people run for cover and start shelling out money to get rid of them. Don't get over-excited about termites, if you do have them. Sure, they exist and they do get into houses and can do considerable damage if they are allowed to stick around, but don't panic just because someone tells you that you have 'em in your house.

If you are worried about termites, spend ten cents and get a copy of the U.S. Government Publication No. A 1.77, entitled "Subterranean Termites, Their Prevention and Control in Buildings."

And while you are waiting for it to arrive, here are a few facts about termites that can help you determine if you have 'em or not. First, flying ants are often mistaken for termites. The difference is that an ant has a tightly constricted waist, a "wasp waist," while the body of a termite is straight. Second, one pair of wings on flying ants is much longer than the other, while the wings of a termite are of about equal length.

The termite "worker" who does the damage has no wings and can't stand light. The termite nest is in damp ground, and the worker must be able to go from the nest to the wooden members of the house or to woodwork without being exposed to light. If he can't reach his goal by going underground, he'll build little earthen tunnels up the foundation walls from ground to where the wood is. If you find these little tunnels—they are about ¼-inch thick— you have some termites.

There are reputable firms in most localities that specialize in exterminating termites, and they will give you a guarantee on the job. There are also some shady, door-to-door salesmen types to avoid. Check with your County

Agent, real estate broker, or local banker for names of reliable outfits.

The way to exterminate termites is to poison the ground around the house so that they can't get from their nests to the woodwork. If you are willing to take the time, you can buy the necessary poisons and get rid of the termites yourself, but it's better to use a professional for this job.

Carpenter Ants: These are large, black ants which will damage wood, especially if it is in direct contact with the ground. You can get rid of them by dusting the area where they are at work, and their nest, with a ten percent chlordane dust.

Fuel Oil Delivery: If you use oil for heating, it has to be delivered to the oil storage tank, which may be in the basement or underground. Most oil companies today deliver automatically. They keep a record of the number of degree days and can judge pretty accurately when you need more oil. If you deal with one of these firms, you don't ever have to worry about running out of oil, but if your oil delivery concern doesn't have automatic delivery, you'll have to keep an eye on the fuel oil gauge and order oil when you need it. The larger fuel oil delivery outfits have service departments that will maintain and adjust your equipment and also fix it if it breaks down. We've found that their service is generally excellent.

Bottled Gas: If you have a gas kitchen range or hot-water heater, they will run on bottled gas. There are two types of systems, and you should know which one you have. With one system there are two tanks, and when one is empty there will often be a peculiar odor when you turn on the gas. This is to let you know that one tank is about empty. There will also be some sort of gauge or indicator near a kitchen window or by the tanks that tells you when you are on the reserve tank. This is the time to call the local bottled gas outfit and get another tank. With the other type of system there may be only one tank and a meter which measures the amount of gas you use. The tank or tanks are filled at regular intervals from a large tank truck, and you don't have to worry about having to order it. It's all done automatically. If you have this system, tell the gas company the size of your family, and how much roasting and baking you plan to do, so that they can gauge about how much gas you are likely to use and how often they should come around.

Garbage: In most rural communities there will be a firm that will pick up your garbage and trash once a week or so at a nominal charge. In these parts it runs about $2.50 a month for one pickup a week. However, in some areas you'll have to haul the stuff to the dump yourself. Most towns have a garbage dump which will not only handle garbage but all manner of trash, junk, and brush. In any event, you'll need to have several large garbage containers with tight-fitting lids so that dogs and other animals won't be able to get at the garbage and scatter it all over the backyard.

chapter **14**

THE WOMAN
WITHOUT A PARTNER

The widowed, unmarried, or divorced woman living in the country in her own house has the same basic problem as her male counterpart—there is only one of her. This means that unless she has children old enough to be of real help, she has to do just about everything herself. She not only has to be the cook and housekeeper but also the yardwoman, handywoman, painter, chauffeur, and all the rest of it. Better keep this in mind when you go out shopping for a country house.

If you are going to be pretty much on your own, look for the kind of house and grounds that you can handle with moderate ease by yourself. A big, old, rambling, run-down house may be loaded with charm, and your friends may say they'll be on hand to help you fix it up and keep it going, but don't believe them. Unless you can afford to have it put in prime condition and hire someone to keep it that way, you are much better off to buy a smaller, newer house, without so much charm but with fewer problems. Those big, old houses were built for families where there were a lot of willing hands to help keep them going. Your single pair of hands, no matter how willing, just can't do the job. And there aren't enough hours in the day, for that matter.

There are other factors about the house that you should consider. If you plan on maintaining the place more or less by yourself, with a minimum of outside help, then you definitely want a house that doesn't require a lot of just plain brute strength to maintain. For example, it takes brute strength to handle the old-fashioned woodframe window screen and storm sash. It doesn't, if the house has the combination-type screen and storm sash. It takes a lot of muscle to handle a long, extension ladder so that you can paint the outside of a two-story house, clean the gutters, or secure a loose shutter. It doesn't take so much to handle the stepladder which is adequate for these jobs if the house has only one story. It also takes considerable muscle to repair a stone wall, clean out heavy underbrush, and shore up a tottering outbuilding.

Another reason why, as a woman, you shouldn't try to take on too much house is that you may find it hard to get a mortgage loan. That's right, Women's Lib notwithstanding, many lenders still take a dim view of lending money to a single woman to buy a house, because they don't feel that she has the strength to maintain it. She can be as strong as an ox with a degree in engineering and architecture, and it still won't make much difference to some of them. The same lender wouldn't give a second thought to lending money to some lazy slob with a bad back who can't even tie his own shoelaces and who might not know the difference between a screwdriver and adjustable wrench. But he, after all, is a man, and a man just naturally knows how to take care of a house. Or so it is said.

In any event, a woman has a better chance of getting a favorable mortgage loan if she is after a new, small house and not a big, rambling monster.

The location of the house is also important. There are some single men and women living in houses that are way off in left field, miles from the nearest neighbors, and they still find life just fine. But we don't recommend it. Aside from the fact that it can get lonely in the country if you go a few days without seeing another human being, it's darn nice to have neighbors close at hand if you get in a jam or have an accident.

In the country, neighbors are about the first people you turn to when you have troubles, and if there aren't any about, you've got a real problem. Ever since we met the rich, elderly lady who had to spend an entire weekend trapped in the private elevator of her town house, we've been firm believers in having neighbors within shouting distance. And if you have kids, it's awfully nice if there is a neighbor who might keep an eye on them for a while if you have to do some shopping.

A woman with her own house has another set of special problems, simply because she is a woman. This is the attitude on the part of many men that when it comes to mechanical things, a woman just can't be taken too seriously. For example, if there is a local power failure and a man calls up and says there's no power in his house, the power company will usually take his word for it and send someone out to see what's the trouble. But if a woman calls up, the power people will ask a lot of foolish questions like "Did you turn on any of the lights, dear, to make sure that you don't have electricity?" or "Why don't you go down and see if a fuse has blown?" When the heat in the house goes off and a woman calls up the service department they'll ask "Are you sure?" (As if you aren't smart enough to be sure you are cold.) And there is always "Did you turn up the thermostat?" But when a man calls, they'll take his word that the house is cold and assume that he checked the thermostat, which he may or may not have done, depending on how smart he is.

You get this sort of nonsense in one way or another all the time. Hardware stores, unless you have a note from your husband, often take an amused attitude toward your requests, and the average clerk in a lumber yard doesn't believe that women are qualified to buy anything except picture molding.

You do have a problem here, because the chances are

that you really don't know all you should about many of the things you'll have to deal with to keep your country house going. It's not your fault. It's the fault of the system. For some reason little girls are seldom taught that to tighten a screw or a bolt, you turn it clockwise, and to loosen it, you turn it counterclockwise. No one bothers to tell a woman that if she uses a pair of pliers on a nut, they'll probably slip and tear up the shoulders on the nut, but if she uses an adjustable wrench she won't have any trouble. No one has ever told her that green lumber is almost impossible to cut, even with a sharp saw, that the size screwdriver to use depends on the size screw, therefore, you need an assortment of screwdrivers—not just one—or that if you want to put a screw into a piece of wood, you should first drill a pilot hole in the wood just a hair smaller than the diameter of the screw. Of course, there are a lot of grown men who don't know any of this either, but most of them do, to one degree or another. And anyway, they are men and can get away without knowing the score; as a woman you can't. So you had better learn the rules.

First of all, if you are going to live in the country and keep your house operating smoothly, you are going to need some tools. In the chapter on "Tools and Equipment" we give a basic list of hand tools. This is just what you should get, including the electric drill. Get good quality tools at the stores we suggest. Don't settle for the "five and dime" stuff usually sold to women. These are just glorified toys and practically useless. If you have never been able to drive a nail straight, the chances are that you had a toy hammer and a cheap nail that would bend even in a stiff breeze. Get some good tools and take good care of them as you do your favorite paring knife or electric blender.

Learn how to use the tools. There are a lot of excellent books written on this subject. One of the best is the *Stanley Tool Guide*. It costs fifty cents, and you can get a copy from Stanley Tools, New Britain, Connecticut 06050.

Get hold of a few pieces of scrap lumber, and some nails and screws, so you can practice a bit to develop your skills. You'll find that hand tools are quite easy to use once you get the knack and know what you are doing. If you have a carpenter working around your house, spend a little time watching how he works with tools. We know of one woman who hired a carpenter for a couple of hours just to teach her the proper use of carpentry tools, and it turned out to be one of the best investments she ever made.

You should also get hold of a few books on home repair and maintenance. There are a fair number of these on the market, and while none of them ever gives all the information you need, if you have several, you'll have a pretty good idea of what home maintenance is all about, why sometimes things don't work right, and what you can do about it yourself. But be sure that you get the kind of books that deal with the basic home repair and maintenance problems and not those that go out into the wild blue yonder showing you in photographs how to build your own sunken bathtub or how to add a wing to your house. You need books that will help you solve the real problems of running a house: how to fasten things on plaster or masonry walls, how to fix a leaky faucet, what you can do when the oil burner doesn't work, or what to do with a sticking door or window. And you want a book that will give you information such as the various types and sizes of nails and screws and how to decide which to use, what sort of adhesive to use to fix a loose piece of wall tile, and what to do about the rust spots on outdoor iron furniture. A good home repair book will also tell you how to avoid trouble by attending to things before you have a crisis. We've found the *New York Times Complete Manual of Home Repair*, by Bernard Gladstone, to be good. Another book you'll find helpful is Stanley Schuler's *How to Fix Almost Everything*. And there are a couple of Hubbard's books that you might also find valuable—

Money Saving Home Maintenance and *How To Paint Anything.*

As you read, you will become familiar with hardware, paint, and carpentry terminology. Learn the difference between a finishing nail, a common nail, and a screw drive nail and learn which kind to use and when. Learn the different grades of lumber and when you can get by with using the lower and cheaper grades and when to use the expensive kind. Use the books to help you learn about your house: that you have a circuit breaker rather than a fuse box, that you have a 120 volt service entrance and not 240 volts, and what that means as far as the kind of electrical equipment you can use. Learn that the gadget set into a pit in the basement is a sump pump which pumps water out if the basement ever starts to flood. Do all the homework you can before you find yourself being tested.

After you have done your required reading, go down to the local hardware, paint store, and lumber yard and browse around a bit. The more familiar you are with the merchandise, the easier it will be to know what you want, so that you get what you want and not something that the clerk may decide you want because you are a woman.

You can't, of course, learn everything from books. A lot of things you will just pick up on your own. One of the best sources will be the mechanics who come to do the various jobs that you can't handle yourself. You'll find that country carpenters, plumbers, electricians, heating servicemen, and so forth, are often quite pleased to display their special knowledge, and if you ask them a few questions, they'll tell you a lot of things about your house and equipment and how to fix many things yourself. Don't bug them, though, especially until they've finished doing what they came to do, and don't try to cross-examine the surly type.

Your Social Life: You may find that you can have a lot more active social life as a lone woman in the country than in the city. In fact, it's sometimes much easier for a single woman without children to get to know people than a woman with a husband and children, because while the married woman is pretty much tied down in the evenings, the single person can get out and around. There are a lot of things going on in the country, and anyone who has some time to help out is usually welcomed. Politics is just one area. Churches are usually pretty active, not to mention all sorts of clubs and organizations, such as the local historical society, friends of the library, garden club, ecology and conservation groups, and what have you. These organizations usually have evening meetings—at homes of members as well as in local meeting halls—and it's a quick and simple way to meet people and make friends.

Entertaining in the country is not as formal or as highly organized as in the city or the suburbs. The country host or hostess is not so set on having an equal number of men and women for a dinner or a party. There are often a few extra men or a few extra women. And you don't find as much emphasis on "couples" as in the suburbs or city. Also, since the crime rate is lower in the country, you will probably feel a lot safer going out at night, especially if you have a dog to guard your house and welcome you home.

chapter 15

YOUR TIME CYCLE
—AND NATURE'S

In the country, time belongs more to nature than to people. The day begins at dawn and ends at dusk. It is a timetable set by crops and by animals, and for a time in the past when there were no electric lights, no central heat, and few outside activities. One went to bed shortly after dark, and the best place to be on a frosty winter's night was in a warm bed, preferably with a warm body beside you.

You will find that the day still begins pretty early in the country. By seven o'clock or so, many people are already hard at work—not just starting off for work as they may be doing in the city or the suburbs. Farmers, of course, always have been and still are early risers. A dairy farmer's day may start before five o'clock, winter and summer, seven days a week. By the time the average city office worker finally gets down to business, the farmer and his family have put in four or five hours of solid hard work.

Farmers are not the only early risers. If your neighbor works in a factory, he also may have to get going pretty early in the morning. Many industry whistles still blow at seven o'clock. Carpenters, masons, lumberjacks, fishermen, etc., who work outdoors and who depend on natural light, are also early risers. About the heaviest traffic we get on the road in front of our house is between six-thirty and seven in the morning.

Country families with school-age children start the day pretty early, because the school bus will hit certain areas before the sun is up. This means the kids have to be up, dressed, fed, and out by the side of the road—rain or shine—often before seven o'clock. This could be you, too.

The community also gets an early start. Banks and stores open their doors before their city cousins do, and they also close them earlier. In the country it's pretty hard to find anything open—drug stores, service stations, even restaurants—after eight o'clock or so in the evening.

Getting up early means not only going to bed earlier but adjusting to a different schedule for meals. Lunch is around noon, and supper may be around five-thirty or six o'clock. And most country activities are planned to fit this schedule. Public and private meetings often begin at seven or at the latest eight o'clock. Many local movie houses have only one showing, and that goes on at seven or eight o'clock. Everyone will have had supper by then, and people can still get home and be in bed on time. For some city people, the very idea of eating dinner at six o'clock— "why it's not even time for cocktails!"—can come as something of a shock. But if you want to participate in community activities, you'll have to adjust.

Going to bed with the chickens and getting up with the birds is not all that bad, once you get used to it. And you may want to (perhaps feel you have to) get up early seven days a week, fifty-two weeks of the year, because there are so many things that need doing, or so you think. In the country it isn't too difficult to get involved in so many things that you begin to feel that there aren't enough hours in the day, and you may feel somewhat overwhelmed by it all. The beginner often bites off more than he or she can comfortably chew: too much garden, too much attention to the house and grounds, too many different projects, too many weekend guests from the city, and too many community activities. And then all of a sudden, there is no time to enjoy some of the real pleasures of country living: taking a long walk in the woods in search of wildflowers, sitting quietly by a window watching some birds against a snowy background, or just taking a nap in a hammock on a summer afternoon.

Don't get uptight, if you want to enjoy living in the country. You will notice that people who are born and raised there never seem to be in a flap the way so many city people are, in spite of the fact that they, too, have a lot of things to do every day. In fact, many country people seem so relaxed about life that city people have been known to call them "shiftless." It's not that they are shiftless, but out of necessity, they've learned to take things in their stride. They don't feel guilty if some days the housework doesn't get done, if the yard isn't tidy, if maybe the house can stand a coat of paint, or an unused barn is apparently falling apart. As a rule they attend to the essentials promptly, but they don't worry about the nonessentials, because if they did, they would be working twenty-four hours a day.

Country people have learned how to conserve their time and their money. You'll find that they wait until all the leaves are off the trees before they get around to raking, so they only have to do the job one time. If one side of the house needs paint badly, they'll paint that side and let the rest go until it absolutely has to be taken care of. And you won't find them joining every local organization around. They'll join the ones they are truly interested in, but not usually because they want to meet new friends or need something to do with their time.

But they do make time to enjoy life, especially such pleasures as passing the time of day with a friend at the local grocery store or service station, having their say at meetings, going fishing, or hunting, taking the kids on a picnic or to the country fair, or even to Disneyland, if they can afford it. They keep up with the times—take trips and vacations whenever they can—and, in general, seem to have much more fun than a lot of city people.

An active social life can eat up valuable time. Most born-and-bred country people pretty much keep it to a minimum. They don't go in much for time-wasting "kaffee klatsches," brunches, lunches, and cocktail parties. If friends come over, it's on a Saturday night, not during the week. Sunday dinner is still a big event in the country, and that's when the clans gather from near and far, including sisters, cousins, and aunts.

You, too, will do well to avoid the cocktail circuit, if there is one, for they can be a great waste of time. There is nothing that can kill the best part of a summer afternoon more easily than sitting around over a few drinks. Cocktails are pretty much a city import; country people have better things to do with their afternoons. Brunches are also big time killers, especially if liquor is included.

The wrong kind of weekend guests are something else to avoid if you have a lot of things that need doing. There are two kinds of guests—the workers and the drones—and the drones are the wrong kind, except for special seasons. Worker guests, even if they are city bred, will earn their board and keep by helping out with the house and outside work. And if you don't have any work for them, they can entertain themselves and leave you free to attend to your chores. Drone guests are absolutely useless. Either they can't do anything or they won't do anything, and so you end up having to spend your precious time entertaining them. The only time to invite drone weekend guests is in the winter when you don't have much to do and have the time to sit around the fire and talk.

In the country you'll be far more aware of the seasons than you ever were in the city. You may have thought you were glad to see spring in the past, but you have no idea how much you welcome it in the country after a long hard winter.

Spring and summer are the work seasons in the country. When city people are getting away on vacations, country families have to stick pretty close to home base, because this is the time when they have to make a major portion of their yearly income—unless they live in ski country or the tropics, where the reverse is true. Whether they are farmers, resort owners, shopkeepers, contractors, fishermen, or run a garden center, these are the seasons when they work hardest. And how well they do in these months is going to affect how well they are going to live for the rest of the year.

Spring and summer will be busy months for you, too. Spring can be the hardest time to get people to help you. School isn't out, so that means there are few local kids who have time to give you a helping hand. It's a busy time for building, which means it's hard to latch onto a carpenter, plumber, or mason. It's the time when everyone wants to freshen up the house, so painters are as scarce as hen's teeth. People are busy putting in their gardens, so it's doubtful if you can get anyone to help you with yours, at least not at any bargain price. And in many sections of the country, spring means the beginning of the fishing and golf season, and these are a drain on manpower until the fish become scarce and many find that their game is worse this year than last year.

Summer is better for getting outside help. School is out, and there may be quite a few young people around who will do odd jobs for you. But don't count on it. Many of the young people prefer to go after the steady, better paying "glamour" jobs, like being a waitress or bus boy at a local restaurant, working in service stations—girls do it too—or working for a local contractor or shopkeeper. There may not be too many who are interested in doing housework, working in a garden, or watching the kids for you. And unless some kind of economic disaster hits the region, all the building trades will be busy as all get-out. So you may find that you'll be very much on your own all summer.

The country relaxes and has fun in the fall. Fall is harvest time, of course, and county fair time and electioneering time and back-to-school time. It's also summer people-going-back-to-the-city time—only this year you're not among them. Some people feel that fall is the nicest time of all.

You'll find that you will be aware of the change of pace. Things are a bit quieter and slower. The town or village is not as crowded as it was. There isn't much to do about the house and grounds. It's too late to start any extensive outdoor projects and too early to get involved indoors. It's a good time for you to relax and enjoy the country around you. Time to take some day trips and do a little exploring and begin to plan for winter.

Except in very hot climates or where there are winter sports, winter in the country is pretty slow. Anyone who can afford to get away usually does, at least for a few weeks in January or February. There is activity during the holidays—Thanksgiving, Christmas, and New Year's—then things just stop. Country people pretty much hole up and wait for spring. On a farm, winter is the time to repair equipment. In the home, it's the time to start new projects, learn new crafts and skills, read, or just watch TV. Dedicated gardeners, of course, move their operations indoors and flood the house with all manner of growing things, and pore over seed catalogs.

You particularly need something going on through the last few weeks of winter and early spring. These can be the most trying times in the country. It's an in-between season, not winter and not spring. You just have to grit your teeth like everyone else and wait. And then one day it happens. It's spring again, and you'll have to put your half-completed projects away until next winter.

chapter 16

ALL OUTDOORS
—YOUR FIRST GARDEN
AND HOW IT GROWS

Inexperienced gardners all usually make the same mistake when it comes to planting a vegetable garden—they make it too big. So if you've never had a garden before, think small, at least until you've been through your first season. Plant the things you and your family like to eat most, but don't bother to plant such things as potatoes and cooking onions that you can pick up fairly inexpensively at local markets and do not have to be fresh-from-the-garden. Cabbage could be added to this list, too. You can put in a corn patch the following year, if you wish, but if you are lucky enough to be fairly near a farm, garden, or roadside stand where you can get freshly picked corn, you might as well save your energies on this until you know exactly how much space and time you'll want to allocate to your gardening in the future. Later on, you can plant all these things, but right now you want to get your feet off the ground before you fly.

You can buy tomatoes at a nearby farm, but it's really much more rewarding to grow your own, and, of course, a lot cheaper. Until you've become experienced enough to have your own hotbeds or cold frames, so that you can start your plants from seeds in the late winter or early spring, you'll be much better off to buy tomato plants and other seedlings—such as green peppers, eggplant, celery, scallions, lettuce, and most herbs—from a good garden center or farm. They'll be so small when you set them out that you'll be sure they won't ever grow enough to feed you and your family, but especially with tomatoes, you'll be absolutely astounded at how much they will produce. Last summer, we set out a dozen tomato plants, plus six that a neighbor had given us, and we were not only feeding guests and our family of three bounteously for about six weeks, but at the peak of the season, we were giving great basketsful to every friend and neighbor we could find who would accept them, plus supplying friends going back to the city every week. One variety of tomatoes that we particularly like and find very hardy is called "Big Boy."

Sweet, green peppers are not as prolific, but they are beautiful to observe growing. They are perfectly formed from the time you see the first tiny pepper, a dark, glistening green, and they are a joy to watch as they expand from about the size of your little fingernail to fist-sized, crisp maturity. There are several varieties of lettuce that should be included in your salad garden: the crisp and crinkly Bibb; Buttercrunch, a Bibb-type lettuce with thick, crisp and succulent heads; and Salad Bowl, a delicate and delicious rosette-like head with tender, fluffy leaves. Once you've tasted these varieties, you'll never be able to look at a head of Iceberg again; there's just no comparison. Raw spinach makes a marvelous addition to the salad bowl, too, and if you've had nothing but frozen spinach for a long time, you've probably forgotten what fresh, garden spinach tastes like when simply steamed and dressed with butter. (You do have to sow spinach from seed in the early spring, however, and sow again in late summer for fall use, if you wish.)

Bush beans are great for the beginning gardener, too, and these you can plant from seed until midsummer. They grow quickly and abundantly and are fun, especially for children, as you can see progress from day to day. Zucchini squash is also a rapid grower and has pretty yellow blossoms along with luxuriant foliage. Cook both of these vegetables just tender-crisp or serve them raw with coarse salt and, with zucchini, black pepper. By all means plant radishes. These can be sown every few weeks, and after thinning, will chug along at a rapid rate and keep you supplied all summer. Unlike carrots, which seem to take forever—and must be started very early—you can harvest your first crop of radishes in twenty-one to twenty-eight days after you've put the seeds in the ground.

And that may be about all you will want to handle your first time out, especially if you also want to get some flowers in.

If you happen to have bought a place where the previous owners already had a garden, you'll be saved a lot of time and hard work. They will probably have put the garden in the best place, which is, ideally, a sunny spot on a gentle slope for good drainage, and without depressions or hollows, which are apt to become soggy. An east, southeast, or south exposure is best. If the plot is a large one, don't feel that just because it's been under cultivation, you have to utilize the whole thing your first summer. Just stake off what you need and plant the rest with ground cover such as soy beans, which will enrich the soil and keep weeds out.

If there has never been a garden on the property, or if the land has lain fallow and is overgrown with brambles, brush, etc., you're going to have a harder time, and it may take quite a while to get a plot in suitable condition. Your County Agricultural Agent can advise you on this.

How large a plot to stake off for your vegetable garden depends on the size of your family and how self-sufficient you've decided to be, but as we said earlier, keep it small in the beginning unless you want to spend all your time in the garden. If you've decided to go for an all-out "everything" garden despite our warning—including cabbage, onions, turnips, melons, and the whole vegetable roster—

you could go up to a quarter of an acre or more. But if you stick to the "specialty" or beginner's garden, a plot approximately forty feet by seventy-five feet or even smaller, will produce quite a lot. Remember, unless you mulch, you're going to have to cultivate all this ground. Even so, a large garden is still a lot of work.

Before you plant any garden at all, have your soil analyzed by your County Agricultural Agent. He and his staff, and the many free publications you can get through your Cooperative Extension Service, will be of enormous help to you. They will analyze a sampling of your soil (in most states without charge) and tell you exactly what enrichment it needs. Whether it is too acid or too alkaline, too clayey, too sandy, what kind of fertilizer to use, and so on. They can also tell you what to plant in shady areas, what kind of trees will grow on your land, what kind of grass and other ground covers to use, and just about anything else you need to know, including all kinds of animal and insect lore. You will find them cooperative, interested, and courteous, and if you have never dealt with the Department of Agriculture or with the work of the Extension Service and the land-grant (agricultural) state colleges, you'll be really amazed and happy to know that at least some of your tax money is being put to such productive and worthwhile use.

In addition to the help you will get from these fine people, you will also want to have some good reference books on hand. One we have found particularly informative is the *Wise Garden Encyclopedia*, edited by the late L.D.S. Seymour. Another classic, especially for organic gardeners, is the *Encyclopedia of Organic Gardening* by the late J.I. Rodale. And then there's James and Louise Bush-Brown's *America's Garden Book*, another very thorough job. For those who don't have much time to spend on their gardens, there is the *No-Work Garden Book* by Ruth Stout, also published by the Rodale Press. This is a warm, witty, and entertaining book about the all-mulch-method of gardening (also a type of organic gardening) developed by Ruth Stout. It has received high praise in many quarters. We haven't tried her methods yet but are thinking of doing so this spring, at least in some parts of our garden.

Once your soil is analyzed, you will want to work the recommended fertilizer and other nutrients into the soil. This is done with a spading fork, or in a large garden, a tiller. The idea is to aerate and break up the large clods, while working in the organic material. Depending on the kind of soil, your County Agent can tell you how deeply you should work it. When you are ready to plant, the top two or three inches of soil should be raked quite smooth. It does not have to be screened or pulverized but should feel like a coarse powder. Read the instructions on the back of each seed packet, and if they say to plant shallowly, do just that. Many beginning gardeners plant so deeply that the seedlings have a hard time getting to the surface; some never make it. Other, more pessimistic beginners sow too thickly, never quite believing that anything much can happen from so tiny a seed. When growth does begin, the plants are much too close together, which not only wastes seeds but makes it harder to thin the row.

Another mistake that many amateur gardeners make is planting everything at the same time. What this leads to is feast and then a long famine. You'll find in your literature information on how much you can expect to harvest from each row of beans or each mound of corn. Stagger your planting, so that you'll have a fresh crop coming up throughout the growing season, rather than all at once.

You will also find that some crops take a lot longer to mature than others. Some take so long, in fact, that if you don't get them in very early they'll be killed by frost before they are mature. Don't wait until the Fourth of July to put in such slow-maturing crops as carrots or cantaloupe. Get 'em in early.

It's a good idea before you even start a garden to draw up a schedule. Decide which crops you want and then check the time they take to mature. Work back from this and write down the planting schedule, so you'll know that if you want fresh carrots by the early part of July, they'll have to go in the ground the end of April, assuming there is no frost. And then figure out when you can put in the next batch of carrots, so they'll be ready when the first crop has been exhausted, and so on down the line.

You have to keep a constant watch on a vegetable garden, not only to find out if it has suddenly been attacked by destructive insects, but also to know when your crops are ready to be harvested. Your average radish or carrot, for example, will not announce when it is ready to be eaten, and if you leave either in the ground too long, they'll become tough and lose much of their flavor. Tomatoes like to hide at the bottom of the plants, and if you don't search them out and pick them in time, they'll become overripe and spoil. Even corn has to be watched and tested, by pulling away some of the husk, so that it can be picked when at its very best.

Whether you plant from seed or set in growing plants, unless you mulch you will have a weed problem and will have to cultivate regularly. Since we see little point in spending the fine summer hours on weeding, we usually do a first cultivation with a hoe or by hand, depending on the size of the plot, as soon as the seedlings are off to a fair start. We then put down a three- or four-inch layer of organic mulch, such as peat moss, hay, or fine wood shavings, between the rows and around, but not touching, the plants. For acid-loving plants—such as strawberries, azalea, and rhododendron—pine needles or pine shavings are good mulch. Grass clippings are about the finest mulch of all, but we never seem to be able to collect enough to make any difference. In any case, these organic mulches eventually decompose and enrich the soil, and while they're doing that, they keep the soil moist and the weeds down, which makes the whole idea thoroughly worthwhile. Depending on how serious a gardener you turn out to be, you will find out through your reading and other research just which mulches work best for you.

While the location of your garden depends to a large degree on the lay of the land and where it will get the most sunshine and best drainage, it's nice if it can be near the house. Aside from the convenience of being able to pop out of the kitchen to harvest your dinner, and pop in to answer the phone, you can keep an eye on it during the day to discourage rabbits from nibbling or neighboring dogs and cats from making it their headquarters. We have enclosed our vegetable garden with a three-foot chicken wire fence to keep rabbits, woodchucks, raccoons, and an occasional deer out, but we have many friends who don't bother with a fence. Our friend Stanley Schuler, who has written a book called *Gardens Are For Eating*, published by Dial Press, sprinkles dried blood (sounds terrible but it's legal and available at your garden center) around the roots of plants and reports that this keeps rabbits away. Rodale suggests powdered rock phosphate, or an occasional row of onions interplanted with other crops. However, another friend, Mary Anne Guitar, who lives in Redding, was so plagued with woodchucks and other wildlife that she had to build not only a chicken wire fence around her vegetable garden but put a roof of chicken wire on it, besides. (Her garden is quite a distance from the house, incidentally.) While fences are more costly in the beginning, they do pretty well and also provide a framework for pole beans and other climbers, in the bargain.

There are, of course, many insect pests that will get after your growing things, among them cutworms, which feast on your finest tomato plants. Somewhere else in this book we mention a folk remedy which we have never read about anywhere and which a farm friend was kind enough to tip us off to, and that is to lay a barrier of skunk cabbage leaves around each tomato plant, then cover the leaves with a thin layer of earth. It works for us, and we hope it will work for you. Garden slugs, another voracious pest, can be put out of commission permanently by putting shallow pans of stale beer around in the garden. This trick, publicized by Ruth Stout in her newspaper column and books, works famously, and it's really worth the beer to see these greyish, slimy creatures pile up in the pans—out, smashed, stoned, or whatever you call it at your house. We also find that marigolds, those bright and perky blossoms, seem to have a deterrent effect on all sorts of insects, including nematodes and eel worms, and possibly even woodchucks. We happen to like marigolds anyway, especially the dwarf varieties, so we are apt to use them as borders almost anywhere or strew them around in little clumps, wherever it seems a good idea. Don't, by the way, make the mistake of confusing earthworms with troublesome pests like slugs, for they are the best thing that can happen to your soil. They keep it aerated and conditioned, along with providing valuable nitrogen fertilizer when their life span is over. They're shiny and wriggly and brown, with segmented bodies, and can range from microscopic to several inches or more. Be kind to them, and if you dig one up by mistake, put it back.

This brings up the subject of flowers in your first garden, and you should have them, by all means. Part of the fun of moving into an older house is the surprise awaiting you when warm weather brings out whatever perennials, flowering shrubs, and bulbs were put in by your predecessors. Especially in spring, there is nothing more delightful than coming unexpectedly upon a clump of golden daffodils, white narcissus, a few purple crocuses, or some lovely tulips planted by some unknown hand. There's just no telling what you might have inherited along with the trees, peonies, phlox, border chrysanthemums, hardy and colorful day lilies, along with lilac bushes, azalea, mock orange, rose of sharon, and perhaps some rose bushes. But even if you aren't this lucky, or especially if you're not, you will want to put in some annuals to provide color and fragrance all during the growing season.

Some of the most satisfactory annuals for the new or the lazy gardener are petunias, snapdragons, larkspur, the sturdy and vivid zinnias, nasturtiums, lavender-blue ageratum, asters, and the aforementioned dwarf marigolds, plus some poppies and sweet allyssum. As with your vegetable garden, we suggest that until you've gained experience, or have the time and inclination to start your annuals from seeds in the early spring, that you buy the young plants from a good garden center. Usually the people there will be very helpful in answering any questions you may have as to planting techniques, and if you have your garden books near at hand, you can, with a relative minimum of effort—well, it's not all *that* easy—have enough flowers within a very few weeks to not only enjoy outside, but to keep your vases filled all summer and even fairly late into the fall, depending on the length of your growing season.

For tools you'll need a spade, a hand cultivator, a trowel, possibly a hoe, a rake, and gardening gloves. Since most annuals are happiest in full sun, you will have to survey your grounds with that in mind before you dig your flower beds, unless they are already there. All flower beds don't have to be rectangular or square or straight; round ones are attractive, too, as are those that just meander. (However, if you are going to have a separate cutting garden, it will be easier to cultivate if rectangular.) When you've decided where to put your flowers, dig up the soil with a spade, making sure you leave a clean cut along the edges. Depending on the type of soil (and if you've had it analyzed, you'll know) you may want to add a fair amount of clean sand to ensure good drainage, and possibly some peat moss and some well-rotted stable manure, if you can find a farm nearby, or you can probably get it from your garden center. Spread a layer of the manure a couple of inches thick and work it into the soil at least three or four inches with the spade, breaking up any clods as you go along and picking out any large stones, coarse stalks, or twigs. If you're digging into grass, shake the loose soil off the clumps, and break up the compact remainder before you turn it under, as the clods will interfere with your flower roots. Then rake the whole bed nice and smooth. When you plant your annuals, be sure and water them thoroughly, immediately after planting, and every day thereafter until they are well rooted, or unless it rains every day.

Annuals should be kept well mulched, just as your vegetables are, but for most flower beds, we prefer peat moss rather than coarser mulches, because it looks neater and the color is more like that of the earth. Pick off all dead flowers every day, and your plants will bloom continuously. This is especially important with petunias. Don't just pick the head of the flower. Instead, reach down with your fingers or pruner and nip the stem carrying the head at the point where the leaves begin to spread out or divide. This prevents the plant from setting seed and dying after flowering—the natural sequence. The constant picking stimulates the plant to continue to produce new blossoms. Tall and lanky plants should also be pinched off as they grow. This will make them spread out and grow strong and bushy. Don't be afraid to pinch back; it's good for them.

You'll also probably want to have an herb garden, not only for flavorful contributions to your kitchen creations, but for their lovely fragrance. Herbs should not be crowded together, but should be arranged very neatly in precise little rows and clumps. This is not only more attractive, but the plants grow better. Our favorites are sweet basil, both green and the rich dark purple; marjoram; thyme (very fragrant); lemon balm; a bit of sage; rosemary; and again, for fragrance, lavender and verbena. The feathery dill is one of our favorite herbs for flavoring of all kinds, but for some reason, we don't seem to have any luck with it. We're going to keep trying, however. Mint is a delight for many reasons, but we don't like to have it in with our other herbs, because it has a tendency to take over and root all over the place. Instead, we keep it confined to a bed all its own where we can chop it out ruthlessly whenever necessary.

Herbs grow best in a not-too-rich soil, and they like full sun. The soil should be well drained, and, if possible, the whole little garden enclosed by a medium-sized hedge, border of flowering shrubs, or some other attractive plant that can be kept neatly trimmed. This not only gives protection from the wind but makes your herb garden a very special little place. If you don't want to do all this your first season, though, you can always grow a few of your favorites in clay flower pots sunk in the earth in warm months and brought inside the kitchen for winter snipping.

You probably won't have the time your first year to do much about any blackberry or raspberry patches you might find on your property, or even about an asparagus bed—should you be fortunate enough to find an established one on the place—unless you have moved in before the growing season begins. Each requires special cultivation methods which you will want to read up on in your garden books. Just don't, in an excess of zeal to clean up your property, cut them down or raze them by mistake. Properly cared for, they will give you years of delicious eating.

Finally, don't take on too much your first year, you'll have plenty of other things to do.

chapter 17

WILDLIFE
—FRIEND OR FOE?

While you won't run across as many wild creatures in the country as you might have forty or fifty years ago, you can be pretty sure that you'll see more of them than you did in the city. Some of the creatures you'll see will be more or less familiar—rabbits, squirrels, deer, turtles, and frogs. Some, such as opossum, skunk, and woodchuck may be new to you, while others—especially snakes—you may not have encountered at all. You should make it your business to learn as much as you can about all of them, for the more you know, the less anxious you'll be if, for instance, a snake slithers across your path or you hear eerie screechings in the middle of the night. The snake is probably harmless, and the screeching or hooting is probably just a lonesome owl.

A good source of information is your County Agent or the state Department of Agriculture. Both have bulletins and pamphlets on just about everything you're liable to run across, including how to get rid of whatever it is you don't wish to have around. Your local library will also have books with pictures of the various species and so will your garden encyclopedias.

If you haven't had dealings with wild creatures, it's worth pointing out that the majority do not particularly care for human beings and will generally go out of their way to avoid them. This doesn't apply, of course, to such pests as mosquitos, who have a fondness for warm blood, or to ants and some other insects. Nor does it apply to any wild animal who is sick or demented. When any warm-blooded animal—a fox, skunk, raccoon, etc. doesn't run away at the sight of you, he is probably sick, maybe with rabies—and you should get yourself, your children, and your cat or dog inside the house and call the game warden. But otherwise, wild creatures won't bother you unless you bother, scare, or disturb them.

You should also be extremely careful about handling any wild creature, no matter how small or harmless it may seem. Almost any animal will react violently from fear, and can give you a nasty bite or scratch. We once got a bad nip from a baby owl we ran across in the woods. A rabbit can scratch like the devil, and a raccoon can give you a very bad bite.

Reptiles and Amphibians: We might as well start off with snakes, because most people dislike them, are scared to death at the very mention of them, and know very little about them. There are hundreds of different kinds of snakes in this country, but only a few are venomous, and even some of these are by no means deadly. Most of the snakes you are likely to encounter around your house and garden are your friends, whether you know it or not, because they eat insects and small rodents. The minority, the venomous snakes, include the rattlesnake, moccasin, copperhead, and coral.

The trouble with snakes—aside from the fact that most people are revolted and frightened when they see them—is that it's hard to tell the difference between a harmless one and a venomous one, unless you know what to look for and take the time to look. What usually happens is that the snake gets killed.

When it comes to finding out what kinds of snakes you are likely to run into, don't depend on local lore; get information from your County Agent. In a lot of communities it's almost a civic virtue to boast about the venomous snakes around, even though there may not have been any in the vicinity for the past couple of generations.

Harmless snakes make excellent pets, especially for children. They don't require much care once you've learned what they like to eat, and they are very clean and not one bit slimy. A kid who has a snake for a pet will never grow up having herpephobia.

By the way, if you ever do have to kill a snake, strike it hard on the head with a stout stick or on the neck right in back of the head.

Salamanders: These are small, gentle creatures found along ponds, brooks, in the woods, and under stones. They are often called "lizards," which is not correct. They eat insects and are friendly, and as far as we know, are perfectly safe to handle. They make quiet pets.

Turtles: There are many different kinds, and you usually find them in the country around ponds or in the woods. They are, for the most part, shy and pleasant creatures, but you should know which is which and how to handle them, because some—the snapping turtle and the softshell turtle, for example—can give you a nasty nip. In fact, a good-sized snapping turtle can take off a finger as clean as a whistle. We once saw one big fellow a couple of feet long, snap right through the handle of a broom. Lots of people keep the more pleasant-tempered turtles for pets, but before you do this, you might check with your County Agent or health department, because turtles have been found to carry salmonella bacteria.

Lizards: In some sections of the country, you will find true lizards, and the most common one is probably the green Anolis, often called a "chameleon," which it is not. Also included in the lizard family is the misnamed "horned toad," which is not a toad but a lizard. In any event, lizards seem to be friendly, for they eat insects and spiders and leave people pretty much alone, except for the green Anolis, which is so playful that he'll sometimes lose his grip and fall on you quite by accident.

Frogs and Toads: We never met a frog or toad we didn't like. Some live in ponds and some in the garden, and they all eat insects and try to avoid trouble. Toads, by the way, will not give you warts if you handle them, but some do have a rather unpleasant odor. It is always a good idea to wash one's hands after handling them, as the secretion from their skin is irritating to the eyes and mouth. Make your grounds and gardens attractive to frogs and toads, for they will repay you by keeping the mosquito and fly crop down.

Birds: On the whole, you can consider most birds as friends, especially if you are a gardener, because they'll eat up a good many insects and harmful pests. Crows, of course, can be a bother if you are raising corn or grain. A scarecrow is about as effective a way to keep them out of your fields as any, although some farmers shoot them. Crows are terribly smart, however, and can usually outwit most human beings. Owls are good to have around because they, along with hawks, eat small rodents. Whether you want to encourage birds to come around your place by setting up feeding stations is up to you, but you should certainly not discourage them.

Mammals: You may run into all sorts of warm-blooded creatures in and around your property, from tiny field mice to deer. Some of these creatures are very good to have about, some are bad, and some are neither good nor bad—just nice animals.

Rats and Mice: You've got to consider these as foes. Even the pleasant little field mice will eat plant bulbs in your garden and can be a nuisance in the winter when they may come inside the house in search of food. Rats, of course, are very nasty, and you don't want them about. Aside from the damage they do, they also carry disease. The family cat, if it's not too old or too well fed, may be of help in keeping down the mice population, but a cat will seldom tangle with a full-grown rat. A terrier dog will often make a good ratter if he is of a mind to do so, or you can use traps or poisons. Your County Agent is a good source of information on how to handle these rodents.

Moles: You may never see a mole firsthand, but if you find mounds in the lawn and garden made by their tunnels, you'll know you have them. If you want a nice lawn and garden, they have to be considered as foes because of the damage they do to the lawn. Also, mice and other small creatures use the tunnels the moles make so as to get to your roots and bulbs. The best and safest way to get rid of moles is with a mole trap. Don't use poisons, because you'll also kill earthworms, and these are friends.

Rabbits: As far as your garden is concerned, rabbits are definitely foes and do as much damage to plants as almost anything you are likely to run into. About the best way to keep them away from your vegetable garden is to put a fence around it—a good tight fence. There are also many rabbit repellents you can use around the plants, which are pretty effective in keeping these pests away from your crops. Rabbits don't care for the odor of onions, and some people put a row of onions around the garden for this reason.

Skunks: These are friends, because they eat up a lot of insects and even small rodents. They'll also get into your garbage cans and scatter debris all over the place if you aren't careful and forget to put the lid on good and tight. Skunks are nocturnal creatures, and you'll seldom see them, but you will not mistake their particular scent. Skunks, by the way, make good pets if you get them when they are young and have a vet remove the scent glands.

Last summer we had an encounter with a baby skunk. We went into our fenced-in vegetable garden early one morning to pick some tomatoes and almost picked up this little skunk who was curled up in one corner of the garden under a large tomato plant. He had apparently found a way to get into the garden during the night but couldn't find his way out and was caught there at daybreak. We left him alone and left the garden gate open. He didn't move all day, in spite of the fact that we had a couple of hard rain showers. We'd check him from time to time and there he was, curled up, playing dead. But just as soon as it got dark, he took off for home.

By the way, if your dog gets involved with a skunk, he'll come home smelling to high heaven. The way to get rid of the smell is to put the pup in a tub and wash him with tomato juice. Scrub him down with the juice and then rinse him off. It takes a lot of tomato juice to de-skunk a fair-sized dog, but it's worth the effort. And if you ever find a dead skunk in the road killed by a car, don't touch him, even with the toe of your shoe, because you'll get some of his odor on you for sure.

Porcupines: These slow-moving creatures won't be a problem to you unless you go away for an extended period, and they decide to gnaw away at some of the house woodwork. Porcupines, of course, don't throw their quills, as legend has it, but if you get too close to one and it strikes your leg with its tail, you'll end up with a collection of quills in your leg. Dogs love to go after porcupines, and the net result is that the dog ends up with a mouthful of quills. Don't try to remove these yourself. Take the dog to a vet, for this job requires an expert.

Groundhogs: In some sections these are called woodchucks or marmots. They are about the size of a large cat or small dog, and while they don't look it, they can run like blazes when they are scared. We have to consider them as foes, for while they won't hurt you, unless you get your hand too close to their teeth, they dig sizable holes in your lawn and fields. People who raise horses hate them, because if a horse gets a hoof in one of the holes, he may break a leg. Some people find sport in shooting these rodents, but the humane way to get rid of them is a special trap which will not harm them and allows you to take them to some other area, some distance from your property, and let them go free.

We know of one person who has a lot of woodchucks on his property; there are also certain people in the community he does not like. When he traps one of his woodchucks, he sets it free on guess whose property?

Squirrels and Chipmunks: If they get into your house in search of food, these little creatures can be quite a problem. The best way to keep them out is to trim any tree branches that come close to the house, because they'll jump from these to the roof. Also block any holes or openings with masonry, sheet metal, or heavy wire-mesh screening. These little rodents feed on grain, insects, and the eggs of birds. They can be a real problem if you have a bird feeder, for unless you can place it so that they can't reach it, they'll eat up the grain as fast as you can supply it.

Raccoons: This is a friend, in spite of the fact that he is a born bandit, and even looks like one with his black mask around his eyes. He's a born troublemaker too, and about as generally mischievous as any animal or human can be. He is an expert at getting into any place where he might expect to find food. Raccoons are nocturnal animals and are extremely dexterous with their front paws. It doesn't take them long to figure out how to unfasten a latch or a catch on a door. We once turned a flashlight on a big fellow sitting on the limb of a tree. He was pulling up a

wire, paw-over-paw, on the end of which was a bird-feed-
ing station with a nice chunk of suet in it. Raccoons
ordinarily eat small rodents, eggs, frogs, fish, insects,
birds, if they can catch them. If you get a young raccoon,
they can make good pets but can be a lot of trouble if they
are given the run of the house. Raccoons are fierce when
cornered and give even a big dog a very hard time. They
have sharp teeth and claws, and you don't want to fool
with them.

Opossums: This is the only marsupial in North America,
and there isn't much more you can say for them. They are
neither friend nor foe—just not very smart one way or
another. The opossum eats about the same things as the
raccoon and is nocturnal. 'Possum hunting is still popular
in parts of the south, and people who are partial to them
say they are good eating. To our taste, they are much too
greasy.

Deer: A deer on someone else's property is a lovely sight,
but when he comes around your place munching on twigs
and the bark of trees, he becomes something of a nuisance
and a foe, albeit an attractive one. Deer can do considerable damage to crops and trees, which is why many farmers look forward to the hunting season, and even encourage hunters to hunt their property. Deer also make good
eating. It takes a high fence to keep deer out, so if you
have a problem with them, better see your County Agent,
as he may be able to solve your problem, depending on
local laws and customs.

Spiders: There are many different kinds of spiders in this
country. Enough, in fact, to fill a good-sized book. Most
of them are harmless, but there are a few that can give
you a venomous bite. If spiders worry you, and they do a
lot of people, the best advice we can give is to get a listing
of the types of spiders in your area from your County Agent

to find out which ones are bad and which ones are beneficial (they catch flies and other insects), and then avoid messing around with the bad ones. Leave the good ones alone to do their thing. Spiders are more or less in the same boat with snakes—no one really cares much for them.

Scorpions: You run into these in the warmer, and especially dryer, areas of the country. In spite of the fact that they eat insects, you have to figure them as foes, because they can give you a very, very painful and toxic sting with the stinger set on their tails. Better get rid of them by pounding the daylights out of them with a stick or hammer. They have a rugged shell, and hitting them with a folded paper or the bristles of a broom just makes them angry.

Insects: There are literally tens of thousands of different species of insects in this country, and sometimes it seems that you must have a good many of each and every one around your place. Most insects are relatively harmless to humans. There are, of course, certain people who are very allergic to the sting of a bee, wasp, or hornet and sometimes even die from the effect. Anyone with a history of hay fever, asthma, or other allergies, and who lives in an area where wasps and bees are plentiful, would be wise to see an allergy specialist who may advise a course of desensitization shots. But aside from this, the worst any of this group can do to a normal person is to give you a painful sting, if you bother them. Bees, of course, are good to have about because they pollinate flowers, and even wasps and hornets are good because they eat other insects.

Certain other insects are very definitely friends, because while they eat other insects, they don't bother people or gardens. The ladybug and praying mantis are good examples, and because they are predators, are very popular with organic gardeners who encourage them to prosper on their property. In fact there are outfits now that sell lady-bugs and praying mantis eggs by mail.

Some insects, such as ants, don't do much damage themselves (except carpenter ants, which will eat away at the house woodwork if given the chance), but they do spread aphid eggs, and that makes them less than desir-able, because aphids suck vital juices from plants. They also get into the house, especially the kitchen, where they can be a great nuisance. There are two basic kinds of ants you'll find in the house: the small grease-eating ants, and the larger ones that like sugar. If you can locate the ant nest outside, give it a dose of chlordane powder. And to keep them under control inside the house, use some ant traps and don't leave sugar or grease around.

In the warmer climates, you may find the fire-ant. These build conspicuous mounds and are very troublesome to farmers because they give a painful sting. Right now, there doesn't seem to be a sure way to get rid of them, but if you do happen to have them, check with your County Agent to find out the latest suggested solution to the prob-lem.

Mosquitos, of course, are a big nuisance, and so are things like cutworms, gypsy moths, Japanese beetles, grasshoppers, and other insects that do damage in the garden and to trees. If you are troubled with any of these, your County Agent can supply you with the latest way to get rid of them. Your garden center can also advise you and so will your garden encyclopedias.

chapter **18**

SPEND LESS FOR FOOD
AT HARVEST TIMES

Some country people live off the land but don't do much,
if any, of their own gardening or farming. They take advantage of what others grow and raise and what they can
take for the picking. And you can live pretty well this way
without spending a lot of money.

In the country, there are "harvests" scattered throughout the growing seasons—whenever local crops and other
foods are readily available and at low prices. Frozen and
processed foods make many of us forget that there is a
special season of the year for almost everything we eat.
In the spring and early summer, local asparagus and strawberries come on the market, and this is the time when
they taste the best and are also the least expensive. A
little later, local tomatoes begin to appear, along with
beans, carrots, and so forth. Then corn comes into its own,
then cabbage and cauliflower, and finally apples, pears,
squash, and pumpkins. The time to buy and enjoy these
good things is when they are at their very best—at the
peak of the season. It's also the time to think about putting some up, either in the freezer or in jars, for the months
ahead.

You get your best buys in foods by going to the source,
or as close to the source as you can. Many farmers will
have retail stands on their property or, often, just pile a
truck with their produce, park it on the side of the road,

and wait for customers to drive up. You get good bargains in either case. Garden centers are also a good source for low-cost produce as the season progresses, and if you live near a large center, there may be a farmer's market. Here you can find a great variety of vegetables and other food products. It's wise to get there as early in the morning as you can, for then you have the widest selections.

The best place to buy fruits is directly from the orchard, and many will give you a special price if you pick your own. It can make a great family outing—picking your own apples, pears, strawberries, blueberries, or other fruit, and you can't beat the price.

Country food bargains are not limited to produce or to harvest seasons. You can usually find someone in the area who sells fresh eggs right where they are raised. Some friends of ours who run a poultry farm have a roadside stand offering fresh eggs for quite a bit less than they cost at the local store or supermarket. It's a self-service honor system kind of operation. You pick your eggs up off the stand and put your money into the little tin pail.

Shop your local newspaper and you'll probably find several outfits that sell meat wholesale. You buy a half or quarter of a steer, and they'll butcher it for you so you can take the roasts, steaks, ground beef, and whatever else you get and store it in your freezer. Right about now, the outfit in this area is having a special: you buy half a steer (convenient monthly payment plan available, if you wish), and they'll toss in ten pounds of bacon, ten pounds of pork chops, and twenty pounds of hot dogs. Some of these outfits also have frozen food lockers so you can store your meat with them if you don't have a freezer of your own.

You also want to take advantage of some of the more specialized food bargains that may occur in your area. If you live near salt water, there will be certain times of the year when a particular kind of seafood is abundant and inexpensive. The time to eat as well as stock the freezer with salmon, scallops, crayfish, flounder, bass, bluefish, crabs, halibut, mackerel, and red snapper is when they are running, and the best place to buy them is at the dock or at a dockside fish market. We used to do a lot of fishing for bluefish, and we'd get six cents a pound for them at the docks. But after that same fish had traveled twenty miles or so to New York City, it was bringing sixty cents a pound, or more. Today, it's way over a dollar a pound.

A good way to keep up with food bargains is to listen to the local "Farm Hour" on the radio or TV. These come on pretty early in the morning, five o'clock or so, but they are worth getting up to hear. You'll not only learn the going price for various foodstuffs, but what is in short supply, what has been held back because of local weather, and what sort of prices you may expect to pay for certain items in the days or weeks to come. You'll also get about the best weather forecasts, next to the marine ones, that you'll find anywhere.

Some of the best things to eat you don't have to pay for, you just have to pick them. There are still areas where you can find wild fruit—strawberries, blueberries, grapes, huckleberries, beach plums, and so forth. All you need to do is find the spot, have a pail or basket and go to work. You can enjoy some of this bounty right on the spot or take it home to enjoy, but you shouldn't miss the opportunity to put some up as jams and jellies, for the home-preserved is far superior to anything you can find on the grocery store shelf, regardless of price.

If you live near the salt water, you can take advantage of what it can provide, just for your time and effort. Clams are fun to dig, and if the bottom is on the gooey side, you can feel them with your feet and just bend down and pick them up. Crabs are fun to catch either with a net or a trap, and when they are in season, it doesn't take much time to get a basketful. It's fortunate for some of us that mussels have never been too popular in this country, for this means that there are still a lot of them about. They are the easiest of all shellfish to get. Just wait until the tide is low, and then go out and pick them up by the bushel. Before you clam or crab, be sure to check with the local health authorities, though, to make sure the waters are unpolluted.

If you want to get the most out of the "harvests" in your area—vegetables, fish or fowl—put some up for future use. Most of them won't taste quite as good frozen or canned as they will fresh. There is nothing that can beat vegetables right out of the garden or fish right out of the water, but if they have great flavor to start with, they'll still taste pretty good.

Freezing is the most practical way to preserve most foodstuffs. And if you are going into this in a serious way, you should have a decent-sized freezer, so you can put up enough to make it worth your while. If you do have a big freezer loaded with foods, you'd be wise to have a stand-by generator, just in case you have a power failure. You'd hate to see all that food that you spent so much time and effort putting up go down the drain.

Lots of people still prefer to put vegetables up in mason jars rather than freezing them. This is pretty much a matter of personal preference. In our opinion, home-canned vegetables don't taste the same as those that are frozen, but have a completely different flavor. It's not a bad taste, just different. You can get all the information you need on how to freeze and preserve foods from your County Agent, who will supply you with excellent booklets on these subjects.

chapter 19
HOME IS WHERE
THE HEARTH IS

When you live in the country, you almost have to have some sort of working fireplace or woodburning stove in at least one room of the house. You'll want a fire to take the chill off a room on a damp or cool day, and you may even need it for warmth in cold weather, if the heating system goes on the blink. But most important, you want it for the cheer it will provide on some of those dismal, dreary days that do occur in the country. (They occur in the city, too, but you don't notice them as much.)

Fireplaces: If your house has a fireplace, it will do one of two things: it will either smoke every time you light a fire, or it will draw. Even smoky fireplaces can often be fixed without too much trouble or expense. Sometimes the problem is caused by a branch of a tree that is too close to the chimney top or even a TV aerial mounted on the chimney. Either can cause a downdraft that could set a fireplace smoking, and the remedy is simple—trim off the tree branch or move the aerial to some other spot on the roof.

A fireplace can smoke if the chimney is not high enough. The rule book says that it should be at least two feet higher than the peak of the roof or three feet above the top of a flat roof. It won't cost much to extend a chimney a foot or so, if this is the problem.

Another reason a fireplace smokes is that the dimensions are wrong. Sometimes this can be corrected by in-

stalling a metal hood across the top of the fireplace to reduce the height of the opening. Other times it's necesary to
reduce the width. In any event, in most communities there
is a mason who knows his fireplaces, and he can usually
find the cause of the trouble and correct it. If you would
like to know more about fireplaces and chimney design
and construction, get a copy of Farmer's Bulletin No.
1899, *Fireplaces and Chimneys*, from the Superintendent
of Documents, Washington, D.C. 20402. It costs twenty
cents and contains a lot of good information.

A lot of houses, of course, don't have fireplaces or have
nonworking fireplaces. In older houses, you'll often find
the original fireplaces have been sealed up or even removed. All this was probably done a good many years
ago, when rather primitive central heating first came into
existence or when coal- and kerosene-burning stoves began
to be mass produced. Today, it's hard to imagine anyone
ripping out or sealing off a fireplace so as to install a wood
or kerosene stove, but if you were the one who had to cut
and haul the wood, empty the ashes, and tend several
fireplaces every day in cold weather, you'd probably have
done the same thing.

Anyway, if the fireplace or the chimney flue has been
sealed, ask a mason to take a look at it, because it may be
possible to open it up without too great an expense. If the
fireplace has gone, but the chimney remains, you may be
able to tie a new fireplace into it or install a metal prefab
fireplace, a Franklin stove, or a parlor stove. None of
these weigh much, compared to a masonry fireplace, so
they can be installed with relative ease, even on the second
floor of a house.

Fuels: What to burn in your fireplace or stove depends on
what's available locally and what you prefer.

Firewood: This is the favorite for most people, and it's
great if you have enough wood on your place that you can

cut yourself, or if you can buy wood at a decent price. In the country, firewood is usually sold by the cord or half cord or by the truckload, which comes to about a cord. A cord, by the way, is a pile of wood four feet high, four feet wide and eight feet long. The price for a cord will vary, depending on the local conditions. We pay around twenty-five dollars for a cord. When you order, be sure to specify the length you want. For a standard-size fireplace, eighteen-inch or twenty-four inch stuff is fine, but if you have a small prefab fireplace or stove, you may need wood no more than twelve inches long.

Hardwoods are the best kind to get—oak, ash, maple, and hickory. These woods give you a good, hot, long-burning fire and produce a minimum amount of smoke and soot. Avoid softwoods such as pine, balsam, and hemlock, for these burn very fast, give off a lot of smoke and soot, and produce a lot of sparks.

Don't store all your firewood indoors, especially in a heated area, for the logs will become so dry that they'll burn up very quickly, and you may also be bringing insects into the house. Keep a few logs indoors, of course, but pile the major portion outside and cover the top of the pile with boards or a piece of canvas so that they don't get soaking wet.

Coal: Hard coal, such as anthracite, makes a great fire for stoves but can also be used in a fireplace if you buy a coal-burning grate. A coal fire will burn much longer than a wood fire before it requires attention, and it gives off much more heat without smoke. Once you get the knack, you can run your fire right through the night. Some people use both coal and wood. They'll keep a bed of hot coals in the grate and then throw on a log or two when they want a nice blaze.

Cannel Coal: This coal comes in large chunks and also requires a grate. It's good for fireplaces but not for stoves.

It's fun to burn because it does a lot of crackling and produces some interesting colors in the flames.

Newspapers: You can make fireplace logs out of newspapers, and they do very well. What you need to make the logs is a little gadget sold at hardware stores and through mail order houses. It helps you to roll the papers up good and tight so that they'll burn pretty much like logs.

Kindling Wood: If you use kindling wood to start a fire, get softwoods, for these ignite faster than hardwoods. If you don't have any scraps around your place, take a run over to a local lumber yard. They usually have a lot of scrap stuff around that they are glad to get rid of, either for free or for just a little change. Old wood shingles, by the way, are great for kindling. There used to be an old couple around here who used wood shingles as their only fuel to heat the house and also to cook with. They had an old truck and would show up whenever someone was having a new roof installed. They'd pick up all the old shingles and haul them back home. It saved the carpenter or the home owner the job of having to pick them up.

You can, of course, use other methods for starting a fire. There are these little fire starter cubes, or you can use an electric or a butane fire starter. And then there is the antique Cape Cod lighter, a metal rod with a ball on one end made of asbestos or porous clay, which is dipped in kerosene.

Building A Fire In A Fireplace: No two people will build a fire in quite the same manner, but this is our method and it seems to work pretty well. Put a few sheets of crumpled newspaper down and then cover them with a few pieces of thin kindling wood laid in a crisscross pattern. Set two logs across the kindling and then put another log diagonally across them.

Before lighting the fire, be sure that the damper is open. Keep an eye on the fire and don't replace the firescreen until the fire is burning briskly. (But don't leave the room until you put the firescreen back.) A firescreen keeps a good deal of air away from the fire, and when it is just getting underway, it needs all the air it can get.

It will help to keep a fire from smoking when it is first lighted, if, just before you light it, you hold a piece of burning newspaper up near the flue to warm it up and get the draft going.

A fire, even in the best fireplace, will smoke if it is set too near the front of the opening. The rear log should be only about one inch from the rear of the fireplace. A smoldering fire will also tend to smoke, and the remedy here is to jazz it up with some additional wood or maybe some kindling.

A fire will also smoke or burn poorly if there isn't enough air in the room. If there is a tendency to smoke, open a door into the adjoining rooms.

A fire does better if there is a bed of ashes on the hearth. Don't, however, let the ashes accumulate so that the andirons become covered, for they may burn out.

chapter **20**

AUCTIONS, FLEA MARKETS,
AND WHAT HAVE YOU

Buying secondhand articles is a well-established custom in the country. In the city, usually only the very poor, the very young, or the slightly eccentric rich would even consider buying used articles, other than real antiques, but in the country everybody does it, or practically everybody. And why not? If you need a particular piece of furniture, a set of everyday china, some drapery hardware, a hoe, a crowbar, or a twenty-gallon pot, why on earth pay for something new when you can get something just as good as new for a fraction of the price.

You can find some wonderful bargains at country auctions, not to mention barn and garage sales, tag sales, flea markets, and secondhand stores. There are even bargains at some antiques shops, if you are on your toes.

In the country, people shop around not just for bargains, however. It's sort of a form of recreation. When there is a flea market, or a garage or barn sale, it gives a body a chance to get out and see what's going on. You can also spend a while browsing around a secondhand store or local antiques shop, and even if you don't find what you want, ask the dealer to let you know if he ever gets in whatever it is you need. Chances are, he'll find it somewhere, sometime, and call you back. Country auctions, of course, are real outings—especially if they are held outdoors on a nice day. There are hot dogs, hamburgers, cupcakes, and soda pop. There are old friends to sit with, new people to meet, and a chance to see what other people will pay their good money to buy. And who knows, you might find just the table you want at a really good price or an old flintlock shotgun to add to your collection. And there is always the chance, slim but still possible, that you'll get yourself a real bargain—an antique for say forty dollars really worth ten times that, once it's cleaned up. Country auctions can be terribly exciting.

But you've got to be careful. Not everything offered secondhand is a bargain. If it's not an antique, and if you don't know what the article cost new, you might end up paying as much for the used object as for a new one. We've seen secondhand kerosene lanterns selling for more than you'd pay for a brand new one, and cheap pine furniture selling for the same price as new furniture in a store just down the street. You can also take a real beating if you get carried away when the bidding gets hot.

If you are in the market for a lot of ordinary items, such as pots and pans, kitchen chairs, lamps, tools, and so forth, find out what they cost new before you go to the auction circuit. And be very leary of mechanical equipment, such as clocks, power lawn mowers, outboard motors, and so forth. Even if they run at the time you buy them, it doesn't mean they'll run for long, and by the time you have them repaired, you might just as well have bought something new. The same holds true of electrical equipment, such as small appliances, radios, and TV's. Avoid them unless you know how to fix this sort of equipment yourself. Somewhere in our basement is a mighty food mixing machine that we got at a real bargain. It works fine except for one thing: whatever you put into the chopper is immediately and violently rejected. That's the only flaw, but it's a rather serious one.

It's even more important that you know approximate values when you shop for antiques, because there is more money involved than in ordinary used household items.

You can get some idea of prevailing prices by visiting local antiques shops. As a general rule, an antiques dealer will price merchandise at about twice what he paid for it. If he paid someone $50.00 for a piece of cut glass, he'll put it on the shelf for $100. If you can pick up a similar piece of glass somewhere for under $100, you are a little ahead. If you can get it for $50.00, you've got a real bargain.

Anyone seriously interested in buying antiques ought to have some sort of price guide, and a paperback called *Warman's Antiques And Their Current Prices* is pretty good. It is used by many dealers and is published by E. G. Warman Publishing Inc., Uniontown, Pennsylvania 15401. This handy little book contains current prices as well as photographs of the more common antiques you are likely to run across.

Caveat Emptor: This is the watchword for anyone buying used merchandise. It's not so essential when you buy from a reputable antiques dealer (but you won't be getting any bargains either) or at first class auction galleries (and there are not many of them outside of big cities), but otherwise, it's a must.

Carefully examine every object you are interested in buying, for once bought and there is a flaw, it's too bad. And when you are buying a set of something, such as stemware or china, you don't want to just check one piece, you want to carefully inspect each and every piece for cracks, chips, or other flaws.

Flea Markets: These are often sponsored by churches and other organizations to raise money. In the summer they are held outside, and they attract antiques and secondhand dealers from the general area. Most of the objects that you'll find are small—things easily transported by the dealer in his station wagon or minibus. It's a good spot to look for odds and ends, accessories and small pieces, chairs or sidetables. Some flea markets attract dealers with fairly nice items; sometimes all you find is secondhand junk.

Garage and Barn Sales: When a family is going to move, wants to make a little money, or has run out of storage space, they have a barn or garage sale. They fill the place with an assortment of goods, put some price tags on them, hang a few signs on the road, and wait. These sales usually take place on weekends, and you are likely to find almost anything. If it's a barn sale, you might find some useful gardening equipment, or even some items that might be considered antiques. If it's a garage sale, you might not find anything much except some used furniture and household objects. You can pretty well tell just by driving by what you can expect to find. If it's a moderately new house, there may not be much of interest. If it's an old place, with barns and outbuildings, it's worth investigating. Where families have outbuildings, they are likely to store things rather than throw or give them away, and some of the stuff that is in those barns may have been there for a good many years and may be of considerable worth. In these parts, there is a garage sale which, as far as we can figure, has been going on for the past three years. It's in the attached garage of a fairly new house, and we guess that it started out as a legitimate way to get rid of some excess junk. Apparently it was profitable, so the owners invited neighbors to bring their junk over. They sold this off, and now it looks as if they go out and buy stuff from other people's garage sales, mark it up a few dollars or cents and then start all over again. In other words, they're in business.

People are much more knowledgeable about antiques than they used to be, and most people who run these sales are probably smart enough to either hold onto good antiques or to offer them to an antiques dealer or to someone else who will pay a good price. So you're not likely to make any real finds.

Barn and garage sales are also sometimes called "Tag Sales."

Secondhand Stores: These run the gamut from plain old-fashioned junk yards to something pretty close to an antiques shop. In the city you'll find many secondhand stores (thrift shops) run by various charitable organizations, but in the country, they are usually privately run, not for charity, but for profit. Some of them specialize in furniture and some specialize in mechanical odds and ends, or in used building supplies. And some specialize in everything. There's one across the river from us. It's a little building on the side of the road, overflowing with almost anything you could imagine. Automobile parts, marine supplies, farm equipment, furniture, toys, old plumbing and bathroom fixtures, and so on. The owner will apparently buy anything, and as he seems to sell what he buys, he is doing the right thing. Some time ago he bought a dozen solid chestnut side panels from the pews of a church that was being demolished. The only trouble was that they were all from the left side of the pews, so they couldn't be used as side panels for benches or anything of that sort. But eventually he sold them—to us—at fifty cents apiece, and eventually we'll figure out something to use them for, other than as art objects.

In any event, check your secondhand stores, for while you'll probably never find an antique (antiques dealers check these places out first when there is a new delivery), they do have some good buys in other things.

It's OK to haggle with a secondhand dealer if you find something that you really want. They don't have any particular method of pricing—just a feel of what they might expect to get for something—so they'll often shave the price if they can make a sale. If you should ever have something to sell and take it to a secondhand dealer, you can expect him to pay you very little. His whole method is to buy cheap and sell almost as cheap.

Antiques Shops: These will range from what are really "better" secondhand shops to fine establishments dealing in equally fine antiques. Country antiques shops usually have a remarkable mix of almost everything—from the very primitive to the latest thing in Victoriana or sometimes things from a later period. Good buys are not always in the smaller and shabbier shops. But you have to know what you are looking at. Prices tend to be less than for similar things in the city, but usually—just as with everything else—you get what you pay for.

Auctions: These are the places where you are most likely to get good buys. There are several different kinds of auctions you will run into in the country. When the entire contents of an estate are being auctioned off and the weather is mild, the auction will often take place outdoors on the property itself. These are the most fun to go to, and if it's an old farm that has been in the same family for generations, with attics and barns full of stuff, you can make some real buys.

The other kind of auctions are the indoor ones. These may be held at regular intervals in a local auction gallery or put together from time to time by a local auctioneer who hires a large hall—grange hall, Moose Hall, or Veterans' Hall—and does his thing. Sometimes an entire estate will be offered, along with other miscellany, and sometimes it will just be a hodgepodge.

You'll find country auctions advertised in the local papers. They'll also generally list the most important items that are to be included in the sale. You really can't get a very accurate picture just by these ads. There may be only a few good things and the rest utter junk. After you've done the auction circuit for a time, you'll get to know the names of the auctioneers who handle the better quality things, and the ones who handle the junk, but in the beginning, you'll just have to take your chances.

Get to any auction early. They usually allow an hour or so to inspect the items before the bidding begins, and it's essential that you do this. As we said before, in country auctions, most of the stuff goes "as is." If the auctioneer is aware of an obvious flaw, he'll usually point it out, but he'll make it quite clear in the beginning that if you buy and don't like, it's too bad for you. Get there early, look over the field, and when you see something that really interests you, take the time to inspect it thoroughly.

One way not to get stung at an auction is to decide in advance the top amount that you'll pay for a particular item and then stay with this decision. If you decide that twenty dollars is tops, don't go to twenty-one dollars, because before you know it you might be up to thirty dollars. Set your top price, stay with it, and accept the fact that sometimes you are going to lose something that you really want just because you didn't bid another couple of dollars. But in the long run you'll come out better. This is the way antiques dealers operate at auctions. They set a top price on every object they want and don't go beyond it, come hell or high water. If you go to enough auctions in your area and learn to recognize the dealers, you can use this to your advantage. Remember that a dealer will generally set his or her resale price on something by doubling what he paid for it. If you see someone you recognize as a dealer bid on something and then stop when the bidding reaches a certain point, you know he has reached his limit. That's when you should jump in, because if you can get that item for a few dollars above what the dealer was willing to pay, you can figure that it's worth almost twice as much. But first you've got to know who the dealers are and not tag along after someone who doesn't know an antique from a black and white kitten.

A lot of dealers are aware that some people do this, and understandably, can get quite annoyed if the same person does it to them all the time. One dealer we know got so mad at a woman who, to use the dealer's words, "picked my brains at every auction" that, to get back at her, would bid up the price on things she (the dealer) knew were worthless and then, when the price got way up there, stop bidding and leave the "brain picker" with her prize!

You have to watch out for some country auctioneers. Most of them play fair and will recognize every bid, but some play favorites and will pretend that they don't see your bid, so they can knock the item down to one of their friends—often a local dealer. If you run into one of these auctioneers with blinders, let out a good, loud yell when you wave your hand to make a bid.

At most country auctions it's a cash and carry deal. The exceptions are those held in regular auction galleries where they might allow you to return the next day to pick up your things. But with most, you've got to haul them away right then and there, so either have a station wagon or a pickup truck, or don't buy anything too big to fit into the car. Most auctioneers will take personal checks.

chapter 21

LUMBERYARDS, HARDWARE AND PAINT STORES

We suppose that there must be some people in the country who never have dealings with a lumberyard, a paint store, or even a hardware store, but they must be pretty scarce. You'll find that things in and around the house constantly need fixing, or adding to, or replacing, and when they do, the place to head for first is the lumberyard, hardware store, or paint store—not only for the supplies you will need, but for the advice you can get from the clerks on how to do the job, or who you might get to do it for you.

Lumberyards: They sell a lot more than just lumber, of course. A good yard can supply you with just about every kind of building material you may need, from concrete block for foundations to shingles for the roof. They'll handle such things as windows, doors, screens, insulation, drainage pipe, fencing, nails, and flagstone. Some of the newer building-supply houses will also handle appliances, plumbing and electrical equipment, along with tools and hardware items.

If there are several lumberyards in your general area, visit them all and do a little poking around. A lumberyard is a lot like an iceberg, what you see in the office is just the tip of the iceberg—it's what's out in the yard and in the sheds that really counts.

Some yards will have a much wider range of goods than others and dealing with them is a great convenience, because you can get just about everything you need without having to shop around.

You want a yard that will deliver and most do, with the exception of some of the discount outfits that have a strict cash and carry policy. A good many yards don't deliver on Saturdays, and most of them have a minimum order that they will deliver. You really can't expect a lumberyard to send a man and a truck five miles out to your place to drop off a couple of dollars worth of materials.

You should also select a yard where the clerks will help you plan a project, suggest a good solution to your problem, save you money by not letting you buy the most costly materials available, and be generally helpful. A good way to learn whether or not a particular yard takes this approach is to hang around the office on a Saturday morning. At a lot of yards, Saturday morning is "daddy time"—when a lot of people come around with the kids to pick up materials for a weekend building project. It's the time when there are more passenger cars in the parking area than trucks. It won't take you very long to see if the clerks are just writing down orders and ringing up the cash register or saying things like "Hell, Mister, if you're going to paint the shelves, you sure don't want to spend sixty-five cents for clear pine. Take the common; it'll do just as good and only run you twenty-three cents a board foot." Or maybe "Hey Joe, see if you can help this fellow find what he needs out in Shed Three." The kind of lumberyard you want is the kind that will take time with the amateur and is not just interested in the professional carpenter and contractor.

We have found that the most helpful clerks are the old timers, the ones who have been working at a yard for a good many years and have built up a vast storehouse of useful information.

It's a good idea to use a yard where you can have a

charge account. Building materials come high, and it's often very convenient not to have to fork out a few hundred dollars right away, but to have thirty days or so to scrape up the money. It's also handy if you are having someone else do the work for you, because if the materials are ordered from your yard, and under your name, you have a record of what was ordered, the quantity, and the cost. And last but not least, it saves you having to be around to pay the driver when the delivery truck arrives. Lumberyards make deliveries at strange hours—sometimes at the crack of dawn—and you may not be the type who likes to be fumbling around trying to write a check at 6:45 A.M.

How To Use A Lumber Yard: If you know exactly what you want, you can phone in your order, but if you are looking for advice, go around to the yard when they aren't very busy. The early morning is bad, because that's when the clerks are rushed getting out the orders for carpenters and contractors. Late morning is good and so is early afternoon. Saturday mornings are very bad, because as we have already mentioned, this is when a lot of amateurs come around for advice and materials, and when a lot of people just browse around window shopping. A good many yards, by the way, close at noon on Saturdays, and most of them close every day around four in the afternoon.

Don't expect instant delivery from a lumberyard. If it's a small order, they may hold up delivery until there is another to be made in your general area. If it's a large order, they may not have the quantity in stock right at that moment, and it may take a few days to get it in. Last fall we had to wait about two weeks to get delivery on seventeen squares of wood shingles because there had been a pretty bad wind storm in our area a few days before, and a lot of people, in addition to us, needed roofs fixed.

If you need advice or suggestions on a project, bring along a rough plan, or even a picture of what you have in mind, when you talk to the clerk. And have at least some idea of the size of the project in feet or square feet, so he can figure quantities for you. You go to a lumberyard clerk and tell him you need enough boards to floor the attic, and unless you can tell him the length and the width of the space to be covered, he can't figure out what you'll need. Always bring the dimensions of the project involved. If the clerk has this information, he can do the rest.

It may help you in dealing with a lumberyard to learn a little of the language and how quantities are measured.

Most lumber, for example, is priced by the board foot. A board foot is a piece 1″ × 12″ × 12″. As lumber doesn't always come in this convenient size, the clerk transfers the actual size of the lumber involved into board feet, and then figures out the bill. When a clerk quotes you a price by the board foot, ask him to tell you what the price is per running foot. That's something a lot easier to understand.

Wood molding, on the other hand, is priced and sold by the running or linear foot.

Cement is sold by the bag, and a bag contains one cubic foot.

Sand and gravel are sold by the cubic yard.

Wood and asphalt shingles are sold by the bundle and priced by the "square." A square of shingles will cover 100 square feet.

Insulation is sold by the roll or bag.

Gypsum wallbound is often called "Dry Wall" or "Sheetrock." It is priced by the square foot and sold by the sheet. The standard sheet is 4′ × 8′ but there are other sizes available.

Nails are sold by the pound, the package, or by the keg.

The clerk at the lumberyard can usually give you the names of local contractors, carpenters, masons, etc. They may or may not be the best, but you can usually figure that at least their credit rating is OK or else the lumberyard wouldn't be recommending them.

The Hardware Store: This is the spot for small items such as screws, hinges, locks, insect screening, weather stripping, and things of this sort. And a good hardware store should have a lot of new stuff but also carry some of the items of yesterday that can come in handy in case of emergency: kerosene and kerosene lamps, in case of power failure; a hand-operated pump, so you can get water out of the well or pond even if there is no electricity, or the pump has gone on the blink; wood- and coal-burning stoves; stovepipe and some old-fashioned kerosene heaters.

A good old-fashioned country hardware dealer or clerk is another great source of information. If you have moles in the lawn, rabbits in the vegetable garden, squirrels in the attic, or field mice in the pantry, they'll have a remedy. If you want to hang something up, put something together, or fix something, they'll not only be able to figure out what you need from your vague description, but even find exactly what's needed among their vast store of goods and show you how to use it. A good hardware dealer or clerk has an almost unbelievable amount of patience as well as an almost uncanny memory of what they have in the store and where it is. The most amazing experience we ever had along this line was going into a hardware store that was a mass of confusion—stuff piled up on counters, the floor, along the walls—everywhere. We showed the man in the store what we needed as a replacement for a brush out of a portable generator we used for emergency power. He promptly climbed up on top of a pile of stuff on one of the counters, pulled out a drawer in the ceiling-high wall cabinet, and handed us a brush exactly the size and shape we needed.

Unless you have a lot of money or strength of character, don't have a charge account at a hardware store, because it's too easy to let it get out of hand. This is especially true when it comes to tools. It's a lot easier to buy them at a hardware store, and you'll often buy just on impulse, but you'll pay more for them than through a mail-order house. Also, having to go to the trouble to write for something often gives you enough time to decide that maybe you don't really need it after all.

Paint Store: This is the other key outfit you need to keep home and hearth in one piece and in good condition. Many hardware stores have a good paint department, but if you can find an outfit that just specializes in paint, you'll usually get a better selection of products and more expert advice.

Finding People To Do The Work: If there is one thing that most city people who move to the country have in common it is a fear that *if* and *when* they need some work done on their house or property, they are going to be played for a sucker by some local workman and end up paying twice what they should for maybe a bum job. The myth of the unscrupulous country workman taking advantage of the city slicker will probably never die.

You are going to find, however, that country carpenters, masons, plumbers, electricians, and so forth, are just about like all other human beings. Some are more skilled at their trades than others, some are more reliable, some will charge you a little less than others, and some are less inclined to take advantage of you than others. But you flatter yourself if you think that, for the most part, they consider you much different from anyone else. Yours is just another job to get done and get paid for.

You will find relatively few large operations (general contractors) in the country. You will be dealing more with individuals, who will not only come over to estimate on the job, but will also show up to do the work. Our local plumbing outfit, for example, is a father and son operation, with a couple of helpers when needed. Either one may show up in work clothes to do the work involved. The building contractor we use consists of two men—the owner and his brother-in-law. If it's a small job that can be handled by one man, the boss does it himself.

As we've suggested elsewhere in this book, it's a good

idea to get a line on people you may need before you need them. This is especially true with things like plumbing, where you can have a sudden emergency, but it's smart to get an advance list of good people to handle whatever might come up: carpentry, plumbing, wiring, masonry, and so forth.

And the best way to get the names of good local people is to ask other local people whom they use or know about. Ask your neighbors, the people who run the grocery store, the hardware store, and the filling station. Sure, you can save time and just call the first person you find listed under the right classification in the Yellow Pages, and maybe you'll get a great guy, but then again, maybe you won't. Better to get hold of someone who comes recommended to you.

Once you get a few names—assuming that you can get more than one name—the next move, unless it is an emergency, is to get an estimate on what the job is going to cost. You'll read a lot about how important it is to get a firm bid in writing before deciding which man to use and before you give him the go ahead, but this doesn't always work. A lot of country workmen just won't give you a firm bid on a job. They'll give you an estimate, and the final bill may come pretty close to the estimate, but you shouldn't count on it. When you do get a firm bid, it will usually be a good deal higher than any of the estimates, because it has to be padded to cover any problems that might come up—especially with an older house, where unexpected problems arise. Last year we needed a new roof and got hold of two good men to look at the job. One gave us a firm bid of $1,700, and the other gave us an estimate of $1,200. The reason the firm bid was so much higher than the estimate was so that it would cover the possibility that all or most of the roof sheathing would have to be replaced if, when the old shingles were removed, the sheathing turned out to be badly decayed. We went with the $1,200 estimate, taking the chance that the roof sheathing was more or less sound. As it turned out, most of it was, but not all, so the final bill came to $1,400. We still saved $300, but if all the sheathing had needed replacing, we might have had to pay more than $1,700.

Most of your workmen will operate on a "time and materials" basis. You pay them so much per hour, plus materials, which either you or they furnish for the job. With this sort of deal, you want to find out what you are paying per hour for the labor. Generally the boss will get a few dollars more an hour than his helper, but he usually works a lot harder. You also want to get an estimate on what the materials will cost. This shouldn't be too hard to get, and it should be pretty close to the final bill.

The best time of year to get people to do work inside your house is in the winter. In bad weather they can't work outside on new construction, so you won't have as much difficulty in getting the best people as you would in spring, summer, and early fall, when there is a lot of outside work to be done.

Once you line up someone and they start on the job, don't be surprised if they disappear for a day or so. If they are good, and in demand, they probably have several jobs going at the same time, and what they try to do is to keep all their customers moderately happy by giving a day or so to one, then a day or so to another. It can be frustrating if you are in a rush to have the work completed, but that's the way it goes in the country.

Amateur Labor: You can sometimes save a good deal of money by using amateurs or semiprofessionals to do some kinds of work on your property. In our area, for example, there is a group of young, male schoolteachers who paint houses during the summer months. They do a better job than many professional painters and for a lot less. You can get such help with yard work, too, but unless you have seen examples of the person's work, or they come with high recommendations, you are taking a chance with such things as plumbing, carpentry, or electrical work.

chapter 22
TOOLS AND EQUIPMENT

You're going to need some tools in the country. Even if you don't plan any major projects, you'll need basic hand tools to make repairs on the house and help to keep things running. What's more, you need to know how to use them. You will also need certain pieces of equipment: a ladder or stepladder, garden hose, and so forth. But don't do what so many city people who move to the country do and rush down to the local hardware store and buy up every tool and piece of equipment that catches your eye. This is the way to get rid of a wad of money and end up with a lot of stuff that you may have no use for. And there are plenty of ways to spend money on a country place without wasting it on nonessentials. Buy useful tools and equipment, not grown-up playthings like two-ton tractors with AM/FM radios and real headlights. Or at least don't buy these adult toys until you've got the stuff you really need to maintain a country house: a hammer, a good selection of screwdrivers, a pair of pliers, and an adjustable wrench.

Hand Tools: No two experts can agree on just what makes up a basic home-repair tool kit, but here are the ones that we have found to be the most essential and that will take care of about 99 percent of home repair jobs.

1. *Claw hammer:* Get the type with curved rather than straight claws. Hammers come in different weights, so try

several and select the one that feels most comfortable to you.

2. *Handsaw:* A crosscut saw is good for just about all the basic cutting you do around the house. The only time you need a rip saw is when you have to cut boards lengthwise, and this isn't too frequently. You might find you can get by with a combination saw, which consists of a handle and several blades which can be easily interchanged. It's good for all sorts of small work.

3. *Plane:* We've found that the inexpensive block plane is fine for most odd jobs about the house. If you get into cabinet work, you may want to get the larger, smoothing or jack plane, but start out with the block.

4. *Screwdrivers:* You should have several of these in assorted sizes, from small to large. You also need one Phillips screwdriver, which is for screws and bolts with cross slots in the head.

5. *Slip-joint pliers:* Good for all sorts of tightening, loosening, and holding jobs.

6. *Adjustable wrench:* Get an eight-inch one; it's good for just about any work, including some plumbing jobs.

7. *Chisels:* One is enough for a start. Get a ½-inch or ¾-inch-wide blade.

8. *Electric drill:* A portable electric drill is a very versatile tool. Buy the ⅜-inch rather than the smaller ¼-inch. You can use this for drilling in masonry, wood, and metal, and it can handle all sorts of attachments, including a water pump.

These tools will get you going. If you want to pick up a few extra items, get a combination square, some C-clamps, a pair of needlenose pliers, and a utility knife. And as you'll probably need one sooner or later, get a plumber's friend or force cup, which is used to clear stoppages from fixture drains. It's a simple tool, but it works—most of the time.

And you'll need a stepladder and perhaps an extension ladder, so you can reach the upper part of the house. Ladders are priced by the foot, so buy the shortest one that will serve your needs.

Garden Tools: What you need here is going to depend on how extensive your garden is going to be, but for generations, people raised a lot of crops and flowers with just a minimum number of tools—hand tools, at that.

1. *Shovel or spade:* The shovel has a long handle, the spade has a short one. Take your pick. The shovel is better if you have to toss dirt from one place to another; the spade is better for just plain digging. Get one with a pointed, rather than a flat tip.

2. *Hoe:* Not much you can say about this, except that it's essential to have one.

3. *Fork:* Better than a spade or a shovel for breaking up dirt and sod.

4. *Iron rake:* A must.

5. *Grass rake:* Good for grass and leaves.

6. *Wheelbarrow:* Get the metal kind, because you can also use it for mixing mortar and concrete.

7. *Small hand tools:* Trowel, cultivator, and so forth. Good for "on your knees" gardening.

8. *Garden hose:* Get enough so you can use it for washing the car, the house, and maybe even putting out a fire.

9. *Pruners:* A small pair is good for flowers and shrubs. For heavier pruning, get a large pair. The Florian rachet-type pruners, now available at hardware stores, are great.

10. *Lawn mower:* Unless you hire someone to do your lawn, you'll need a mower. The reel types are best for the lawn, but the rotary types are the least expensive.

Among the other tools you might need for outside work are a crowbar, for moving heavy rocks and prying out tree stumps; a mattock, for cutting up thick sod and packed dirt; a pickaxe, if you are going to do a lot of heavy digging; and a sledge hammer for breaking rocks and driving wedges to split up wood.

Good-quality new tools are expensive. The intelligent way to go about getting what you need is to start off with only the basic ones. Never buy a new tool unless you are sure that you will have continued use for it. Shop for the best price when you buy new tools. Buy certain tools secondhand whenever you can. Don't buy—rent—the expensive, specialized tools and equipment.

About the best place we've found to buy new tools is from the Sears Roebuck or Montgomery Ward catalogs. Both of these outfits have a very complete line of tools and equipment. And what they sell is good—often as good as you can find. But to get the best price, you have to order from the catalog, and it is sometimes several weeks before you get delivery. You can also buy the same line at Sears' or Ward's retail stores, but the price is higher than in the catalog. Sears retail stores do have some good specials, however, and these can be worthwhile.

Local hardware stores, lumberyards, and garden supply outfits usually stock the nationally advertised merchandise, and it's usually the most expensive, unless you go to a discount hardware store. On the other hand, these stores are convenient and are where you will normally go when you need a tool or piece of equipment in a hurry. Some of these stores do have "bargain counters" where you can sometimes pick up off-brand stuff for a lot less than you would pay for the name-brand merchandise. The quality isn't always the greatest, so stick to items such as hammers, pliers, and screwdrivers—things without cutting edges.

Some of these outfits have clearance sales in the late summer and fall on garden stuff, and you can get some good buys at this time, if you can wait that long.

You can get some great bargains on secondhand tools if you are willing to shop around and can wait until you find what you want. The place to look is at barn and garage sales, secondhand and junk stores, and country auctions. Just be sure to take a good hard look at what you are buying and also know what it might cost new. No point in buying a used wood plane for $7.50 from some local robber, if you can get a new one for $8.00. Over the years we've picked up many secondhand tools. The ones we prefer are those that are hard to harm by improper use. We have a six-foot crowbar for 75 cents (it's hard to hurt a crowbar), a couple of iron rakes that cost us $1.00 apiece, a $1.50 hoe, and a $2.00 sledgehammer. We also have a four-foot, one-man-two-man saw that was a real bargain at $2.50, because the teeth were sharp and properly set. Normally we stay away from secondhand cutting tools like saws, chisels, and planes, because if the cutting edge is in bad shape, it takes time or money to put it back into shape, and sometimes it can't be done at all. But for other items, you can't beat the secondhand market.

One of the great things that has happened in the last few years is the development of tool rental outfits. In the past, it's been possible to rent certain tools from hardware stores or paint shops, but now the tool rental stores have all sorts of wonderful things under one roof. One of the first things you should do when you move to the country is to check the Yellow Pages under "Tools, Rental," and see if there is a store nearby. If so, visit it, and you'll be amazed at what you can rent and how much work it can save you. You'll find power posthole diggers, power trench diggers, electric or gasoline chain saws, concrete mixers, heavy-duty vacuum cleaners for cleaning the basement, attic, or the hay and straw out of an old barn. There are shredder-chippers which will chew up dead leaves, small tree branches, and other organic debris, so it can be used for compost material or garden mulch. There are power cultivators for getting soil ready for planting; all types of mowers, portable and table; electric saws; plumbing tools; and Lord knows what else. You'll find that the price per day is pretty good.

If you are considering buying a certain piece of equipment, it makes a lot of sense to rent one for a day or so to see how you like it, and if it's something you can really use. You might find, after you've tried it, that it isn't your bag, so all you have to pay is a few days rent, rather than full retail price for something you don't want or don't like. A friend of ours had a longing for a special kind of rotary power saw designed for clearing out small trees and heavy underbrush. He was about to buy one, but someone convinced him that he should rent first, just to see if it worked. It worked, but our friend was terrified when the blade started roaring around. He ran off and left the thing roaring until someone turned it off. Renting tools can save you this sort of thing.

Learning How To Use Tools: When you rent tools, the clerk should tell you how to use the particular piece of equipment, and if he doesn't, insist that he tell you. Aside from the fact that you aren't going to get much for your money if you can't make the thing work, a lot of equipment can be dangerous if you don't know how to operate it. Anything that has moving parts and is power-driven, by either electric or gasoline power, can hurt you or anyone who happens to be around, if you don't know what you are doing. So get complete instructions before you leave the shop.

When You Buy Power Tools: When you buy an electric drill, power lawn mower, or portable electric saw, instructions on use will be included, and often suggestions on other manuals to read to help you become familiar with the piece of equipment. Better do this, because if you aren't careful, you can damage either the equipment or yourself.

With a lot of tools, of course, there are no directions included. When you buy an axe, a handsaw, a screwdriver, or shovel, the manufacturer doesn't usually furnish you with a nice little booklet on how to use his product. You are pretty much on your own.

chapter 23
EMERGENCIES

If you live in the country, you've got to learn to cope with emergencies. Some of them are minor—like the cat having kittens in the coat closet. Some are serious—like the house catching on fire. And some of these emergencies might have been prevented, had you been more careful or known what to expect. Others are acts of God that occur no matter what you do or don't do. You have to learn to deal with them as effectively as you can.

Fire: Next to a bad accident or a sudden, serious illness, this is just about the most awful emergency that can happen. A fire in the country can be especially bad, because the fire department is often a good many miles away, and there is no friendly fire hydrant for the boys to hook their hoses to when they do arrive. They often have to depend entirely on chemical extinguishers, and on the water in the tank truck. But in spite of these handicaps, local volunteer fire departments do a wonderful job, have saved many a house and kept property damage to a minimum. But try to avoid finding out how good your local fire department is by not letting your house catch on fire. Most home fires are caused by accumulations of junk in basements, attics, and so forth, or by faulty wiring, electric appliances, or heating equipment, plus human carelessness and sometimes lightning.

Junk: A lot of trash in the basement, attic, barn, or an outbuilding may not start a fire, but it can certainly turn a spark into one hell of a blaze. And some things, like oily rags and wet hay, can start a fire by spontaneous combustion. So get rid of all the trash and junk, even if you have to pay someone to come in with a truck and haul it to the dump for you.

Faulty Wiring And Electrical Equipment: This is something else you *can* do something about. If you have an old house, by all means have an electrician inspect the wiring to make certain that it is adequate and safe. If the place is covered with extension cords and other makeshift arrangements, get rid of them and have proper wiring installed. We once had a house where about half of the permanent wiring turned out to be telephone wire—good for about 12 volts but not the 120 volts in a house electric system. Our electrician never could figure out why the wiring, along with the house, hadn't burned up. In any event, it certainly should have.

As soon as any piece of electrical equipment starts to act up, either have it fixed or toss it away. In theory, a fuse or circuit breaker is supposed to blow when there is an overload or a short circuit, but it doesn't always happen this way. We know a man who once set a house on fire by turning on a radio that wasn't working properly and then forgetting about it. Half an hour later the entire room was on fire. A few months ago, a neighbor's house caught on fire because one of the kids forgot to turn off an electric blanket in his bedroom, and there was something wrong with the wiring in the blanket. There isn't any particular rule you can follow here, except common sense. We try to remember to *unplug* any electric appliance after we've finished using it. If we just turn off the switch on an appliance, we have that nagging doubt that maybe we didn't turn it all the way off. So watch your electrical equipment. Be sure that it is in firstclass condition and don't depend on fuses or circuit breakers to prevent a fire from a short circuit or overload. Maybe they will and then again, maybe they won't.

Heating Equipment: Modern heating equipment—electric, gas, or oil—has enough safety devices so that it's about as safe as can be, especially if you have it serviced once a year. But a lot of the stuff you find in old country houses doesn't have these protective gadgets and could give you trouble. And often the equipment is installed in such a way that it's almost an open invitation to a fire. We've seen red-hot metal stove pipes supported from ceiling joists by wood brackets; oil burners with no valve to shut off the flow of oil to the burner, should something go wrong; and coal or wood stoves set right up against wood paneling. Have your heating equipment checked out by a competent serviceman or by your fuel company and do what is suggested to make the equipment safe.

Chimneys, too, are another fire hazard. Many of the old ones don't have a clay flue liner—just bricks laid in mortar. In time, the acids in the smoke eat out the mortar and pretty soon there is a gap where a spark can pass from chimney to woodwork. And just to make matters a little worse, you'll often find the wood timbers of a house set right into the chimney bricks. Have a mason check the heating-system chimney, as well as the fireplace itself, and the fireplace chimney. If the chimneys don't have liners, he can coat the inside with mortar, which will seal up the cracks and keep you out of trouble for a good many years. Also have him check the inside of the chimney to see if it is coated with a heavy accumulation of soot. If it is, and you have a hot enough fire going in the fireplace, the soot can start to burn and you have a chimney fire. A chimney fire is not only very dramatic but can be serious. If there are cracks in the chimney, sparks may get to the house woodwork, and sparks shooting out of the top of the chimney can set the roof on fire, if it is made of wood.

Cleaning A Chimney: You may have to do this yourself, or at least supervise the work, because there don't seem to be many chimney sweeps left in this country. Put some rocks into a burlap bag and then fill it with excelsior or straw. Tie it with a strong cord, get on the roof, and lower it down the chimney. Pull it up and down and repeat until you've loosened all the excess soot in the flue. When cleaning a fireplace chimney, always put a drop cloth over the fireplace opening, because if you don't, all the soot is going to float into the room and make a real mess. And needless to say, if you do this job yourself, wear old clothes and work gloves.

Lightning: Some types of terrain seem to attract lightning more than others. By talking with your fire chief, insurance broker, or County Agent, you can find out how much of a problem it may be in your area. If the consensus of opinion is that your property might have a fair chance of getting hit, it might be worth installing lightning rods. This job should be done by professionals. It's not a do-it-yourself project or something that can be handled by the local handyman. All materials used should be approved by the Underwriters' Laboratory, and you should get a guarantee from the installer with a "Master Label" plate. This indicates that the job is correctly designed and installed. And while you are at it, be sure not to overlook large trees or outbuildings, for these, too, can be struck by a bolt. If you have a TV antenna on the roof, disconnect it from the set during a storm. During a bad storm, as you probably know, it's also a good idea not to talk on the telephone, take a bath, stand under a tree or in an open field.

Carelessness: What can we say about carelessness except don't smoke in bed, and if you do, don't fall asleep with a lighted cigarette or cigar in your hand. Well, you can remember to always use a fireplace screen when you have a fire going, never to burn dried Christmas greens in the fireplace, and to always make sure that the damper is open. Also, never try to start a fire with gasoline. Don't burn brush and trash; it not only pollutes the air, but these fires often get out of control, especially if there is any sort of a breeze blowing. We knew a family who had a large field in back of their house, and every April they'd get the urge to burn it off. The fire always got out of control every year, and it took the combined efforts of the fire department and all the neighbors to get the darn thing under control and to save the house and barns. But, the next April, they'd do it all over again.

Dealing With Fires: Assuming that you could have a fire some day, you might as well be prepared to deal with it. First, stick a label with the number of the fire department on your telephone and any extensions. Next, figure out how to get all the members of the family out of the house quickly if it should catch fire. If you live in a two-story house, you should buy a couple of emergency rope ladders. These are particularly valuable if there is only one flight of stairs. If you have children, it is smart to conduct a family fire drill twice a year, or even more frequently, so that every member of the family knows exactly what to do and how to get out of the house, even if they are half asleep.

Fire-Fighting Equipment: Authorities on the subject say that if you have a fire, get everyone out of the house, call the fire department, and then, if you think you can, start trying to put the fire out yourself. The best way to deal with a fire that is feeding on wood, paper, grass, or brush is plenty of water. Keep a garden hose connected to an outside faucet to deal with fires of this type. In the winter, we keep a garden hose connected to a faucet in the basement, so it's handy in case of trouble. Water is the wrong approach if you have an electrical fire, or one feeding on grease, oil, or gasoline. If you turn water on an electrical fire—an appliance that has gone haywire or faulty wiring —you can get a shock that might be fatal. And if you put water on a grease, oil, or gasoline fire, it will spread the fire rather than put it out. What you need for these fires is a chemical extinguisher, and there are plenty of good ones on the market approved by the Underwriters' Laboratories. Read the directions on how to use the equipment and be sure that the units are recharged when indicated and keep them in a place where they will be handy. Oven fires can often be smothered with a liberal dousing of baking soda or salt. Keep a big box of both handy and don't be stingy with it. If someone's clothing catches on fire grab a heavy, wool coat or blanket and wrap the individual in it to smother flames, protecting the face as much as possible. If you're not *sure* the blanket or coat is wool, better not take a chance on a man-made fiber. Instead, use a heavy cotton quilt or bedspread.

As we said before, lack of water can be a serious handicap in fighting a fire in the country, so if there is a good source of water near the house—a pond, swimming pool, or even a shallow well—tell your local fire department about it and the location. Then, if you should happen to have a fire and not be around, they'll know where to go for water. If there is a brook or swamp on the property, you might consider making a water or "fire hole". This is a small artificial pond or shallow depression made by a bulldozer, and it can contain a good deal of water.

Electric Power Failure: How much of an emergency this presents depends on how long it lasts. If the power is out for just a few hours, it's not much more than a slight inconvenience, but if it lasts for a day or more, it can be a real problem. Coping requires some ingenuity, as well as some emergency equipment.

When the power goes off in the country, almost everything in the house stops. You won't have water, because the pump is off. In the winter, you won't have heat. If you use an electric stove, you can't cook, and obviously you won't have any light. Your electric blankets won't keep you warm, and you won't be able to use small appliances, or even the radio or TV, unless they are battery operated. If the power is off for a day or so, food in the refrigerator will begin to spoil, and food in the freezer will thaw.

The best way to deal with a power failure is to assume that sooner or later one is going to occur and be prepared. If you use an electric range, you should have an auxiliary propane or gasoline camp stove so that you can cook and heat water. Keep enough canned foods on hand so you can prepare simple meals without cooking, if necessary. Have a good supply of flashlights in working order, and maybe a few kerosene or gasoline lamps or lanterns. A battery radio is good to have, too. And always keep a reserve supply of firewood for such an emergency.

Having no water is always the big problem. If you get advance warning of a big storm or hurricane—wind, rain, snow, or what have you—make a habit of filling all bathtubs and every large container you can find in the kitchen, before the storm hits. If you do this, you'll have water for cooking, washing up, and flushing the toilets, even if you don't have power for several days. If you have a shallow well, it's smart to install a hand pump, in addition to the electric one, so that you can get water easily if the electric pump is not working.

Lots of country people have standby generators that will provide them with electric power for essentials when there is a power failure. A small portable unit with enough capacity to keep the refrigerator and freezer going and even run the pump will cost around $150.00. A unit capable of providing all the power required for a normal house can cost up to $4,000. Standby equipment of this sort is a must for chicken farmers and those raising animals as a business.

A good way to prepare in advance for an electric power failure is to make a game of it with the entire family. Make a list of everything in the house that will be affected if the power goes off, and then let everyone figure out ways to deal with that particular situation. If the kitchen range is out, what about cooking in the fireplace? Fine, but do you have a reserve supply of wood or charcoal? Do you have a grille or something similar that you can set over the fire to hold pots and pans? No water because the pump is out? Maybe you can get water from a nearby pond or brook. But do you have pails or buckets, and do you have an axe to break through the ice if the pond happens to be frozen over? Play this game, and you'll end up knowing pretty much what you'll need to get along with. Kids, incidentally, usually get a big kick out of blackouts. It's dramatic and cozy, cooking by candlelight over an open fire and going to sleep curled up in a blanket before the fireplace.

Storms, Floods, and Earthquakes: You may run into serious storms in the country. Sometimes it's just a good, hard windstorm, but even these can toss things around outside unless they're tied down. Blizzards, hurricanes, and tornadoes can be serious, especially if you are not prepared for them. You'll get advance warnings on most storms if you listen to local weather reports on your local radio station. City people often don't bother with the local radio station, because sometimes the programs are not so hot, but you should certainly check them for local weather, at least during seasons when violent storms can be expected. And by all means keep a transistor radio turned on during a storm. (This is when a transistor radio really comes in handy.) If the phone is dead, the radio is about the only way you'll know if you should go to the storm cellar when there are tornadoes in the vicinity, or get away from the house if there is danger of flooding from a river or tidal wave. If you aren't sure what kind of natural disasters you might have to face in your area, check with your County Agent. He can tell you what might happen, and what you should do to protect your family, yourself, and your property.

Medical And First Aid: If you don't know emergency first aid, bone up on it! Get a first-aid manual and keep it handy. Know how to treat shock, bleeding, burns, and cuts. Find out how to treat bruises, sprains, how to recognize heart attack symptoms, and what to do for a simple stomachache—no laxatives, please, since it may be an appendix that's kicking up. Have a good first-aid kit handy and keep your local doctor's name and phone number handy, along with the nearest emergency clinic and hospital.

Help! Police: In most small communities there is often no local police force, and when you have trouble you have to call the State Police. Keep the number of the nearest State Police Barracks or the resident State Police officer handy. The police are usually the ones to call in any emergency. If you need an ambulance or can't reach your doctor, call the police. If you don't have a doctor, the police can get one for you. And if you have any other kind of emergency that you can't deal with yourself, the State Police will either help you out or get someone who can.

Accidents: There are probably more ways to get hurt when working and playing around your house in the country than there are in the city. A good many of them can be avoided if you take reasonable care.

First of all, don't overdo. If you aren't used to hard physical labor, you are asking for trouble if you overexert before you get into shape. And maybe you'll never get into the kind of shape to do certain jobs. Our doctor is dead set against any man over forty shoveling snow, unless he shovels snow for at least two hours a day every day of the year.

Most accidents are caused by carelessness. Never work on a ladder, for example, unless you can have one hand free at all times to hold on with. Don't leave such things as equipment and lumber around to stumble over.

Treat any kind of power equipment with a great deal of respect. A lot of people get hurt when using such equipment, because they don't dress properly. Never wear loose or flowing garments. Use common sense when working with machinery. Every year a certain number of people lose a finger or two, because they try to clear a power snow blower with their hands when the motor is running. Others get banged up from small stones being tossed off the blade of a power lawn mower.

We think it's a wise idea, by the way, for all members of the family to get a tetanus shot or booster when they move to the country. It doesn't hurt, and if someone steps on a rusty nail or gets a deep cut from a piece of equipment, he or she is protected. Even so, if something like this does happen, check with your doctor.

It's impossible to list all the emergencies that might occur in the country, but here are a few, along with ways to deal with them.

Flooded Basement: In many areas the local fire department will come and pump it out for you. There usually won't be a charge, but if you'd like to make a small contribution to the fire department, it will probably be accepted. If the fire department doesn't do this sort of thing, call a plumber or a general contractor, as they usually have portable pumping equipment.

No Heat: When this occurs during a power failure, conserve the heat inside the house as best you can. Don't allow doors and windows to be opened, unless absolutely essential. If the house is kept closed, it will keep warm enough for a day or so to prevent the pipes from freezing in below-freezing weather. But if the temperature inside the house gets below forty degrees, be prepared to drain the plumbing, unless you are sure of getting heat in a matter of hours. You might also check with local contractors to see if they have a portable generator that could be used to operate the system so the house could be warmed up. Burning a good hot fire in the fireplace will help keep a house warm, but it has to be a really good fire. If it's just a little one, you'll lose more heat up the flue than you gain.

Strange Dog About The Property: Don't attempt to cope with a strange dog or any other wild or tame animal that seems to be acting peculiarly, for it may be rabid. Rabies, unfortunately, has been on the increase in this country in the last few years and can affect all kinds of animals, including squirrels, bats, and man—if bitten by a rabid animal. The last thing you want to do is to have to go through the extremely unpleasant series of shots that are given against rabies. The only thing worse is not having the shots, should they be necessary. Keep children and pets inside and call the dog warden, game warden, or State Police.

Whether you live in the city or in the country, you are going to encounter emergencies of one sort or another, because they are a part of life. No one can be totally safe anywhere. For our part, we'll take the country brand.

INDEX